MW01233483

Serving Up Memory

Stories, Poems, & Recipes

WITHDRAWN

PROOF

Serving up Memory

Available Oct. 30, 2014

at

Amazon & Independent Book Stores

Parents Are Responsible
For Children's Choices

Washington County Public Library
1444 Jackson Avenue
Chipley, FL 32428

Serving Up Memory

Stories, Poetry, & Recipes

Camden Writers

Camden Chapter

South Carolina Writers' Workshop

Waxing Crescent Press

Copyright © 2014 Camden Chapter, South Carolina Writers Workshop.

Senior Editor, Kathryn Etters Lovatt

Internal Book Design, Jayne Padgett Bowers

No part of this anthology may be reproduced in any form without permission from Camden Writers at camdenchapter@hotmail.com.

Camden writers are members of the Camden Chapter of the South Carolina Writers' Workshop (www.myscww.org), which is funded in part by the South Carolina Arts Commission.

ISBN-13: 978-0692313176

ISBN-10: 0692313176

Cover Photo and Design, Rick and Paddy Bell

Printed in the United States of America

Southerners love a good tale. They are born reciters, great memory retainers, diary keepers, letter exchangers...great talkers.

Eudora Welty

We dedicate this book to all those, Southern or not, who share their stories and inspire us to write them down.

Contents

Lived in Full

Ties that Bind

More Than Fruitcake

The Standing People

We and the Land are One

Angels in Unlikely Places

PREFACE

In 2007, a small group of writers met at the Kershaw County Library to discuss forming a critique group. Before the evening ended, a number of us made a commitment to gather once a month in order to read, to review and help refine one another's work. Some of us were beginners, others seasoned writers, but we all wanted the same thing: a supportive community that would encourage and challenge us in our craft. Under the auspices of the South Carolina Writers' Workshop, we established the Camden Chapter, although many of our chapter members come to us from other towns and counties.

For seven years, we have continued to meet and expand. In order to accommodate diverse schedules, there is now both a morning and an evening meeting every month. We are proud to have published books, stories and essays as well as to have won numerous awards, but with or without accolades, we write on. Often, we bring to the table stories close to our hearts, writing down our own memories or those of others, sometimes writing out of a desire to preserve what has moved us. That perhaps is the common thread that runs through *Serving up Memory*.

This anthology is an example not only of our individual work but also of our communal work. It is as much a product of cooperation as it is inspiration, and every book like this one—written, revised and published by a very few—has a driving force. In this instance, the one person with the passion and the energy to take on such a project was Jayne Padgett Bowers. She introduced the idea, reintroduced it and volunteered to slog through the mystifying technical demands.

The Camden Writers are grateful to Jayne for her vision as this book went from idea to possibility to reality and, now, into your hands.

Kathryn Etters Lovatt
Douglas Wyant
Founding Members

Kendall Mill

LIVED IN FULL

Life is either a daring adventure or nothing at all.
Helen Keller

Camden Writers

Lived In Full
Kathryn Etters Lovatt

People who keep journals have life twice.
Jessamyn West

In the fall of 2011, when Mary Alden Carrison and I first met, she was already preparing to leave Camden. She had lived alone for 20 years, but now, when she was 89 and losing her eyesight, she wanted to be closer to her children. Two of her three sons resided with their families in North Carolina. She hosted a luncheon, reminding guests the occasion was strictly a celebration.

"All fun," she insisted, "no tears."

Not many weeks after, she began packing for what she called "my new adventure," but, by her oldest son's account, every facet of his mother's life has contained an element of adventure.

"To borrow one of her expressions," said Henry III, "she undertook projects 'like she was killing snakes.'"

"She's always been curious, and she was always learning, whether from books or travel or from meeting new people. She was a 'go-er,' too. 'Don't invite me unless you want me,' she would say, 'because, lo and behold, I'll be there!'"

His mother would have made an excellent farmer, he added. "Or better yet, she could have operated a wild flower nursery." He recalled that Mary Alden could "grow almost anything, almost anywhere. Mother probably had more books on Carolina native plants than the Camden library."

When she discovered that I was a writer, she told me that "reading, writing and gardening were the only things I ever really wanted to do."

But she was once an inveterate collector, too. Seashells and fossils, old keys, beach glass, antique silver, foreign coins, and unusual shaped seeds were among the material things she gathered, but she also had a keen interest in family history. Mary Alden interviewed and taped the stories of many of her older relatives. Keeping accounts of earlier times was always dear to her, and the importance of her own past, and her record of it, does not escape her now. She wrote down much of her life as she lived it.

"I've kept a journal since forever," she said. "I have forty or fifty built up. Now I'm trying to figure out what to do with them."

When Mary Alden faced the decision many diarists must—to pass their volumes along or feed them to a fire—neither option suited her.

"These aren't for publication, because, along with everything else, my frustrations are in there," confided Mary Alden. "If I got mad at somebody, for instance, or felt irritated with Henry, I put it on paper and got it off my chest."

That would be Henry George Carrison, Jr., her late husband.

"They are, you understand, *feelings* journals. Private. But they reflect a life and time in history, too."

Mary Alden's journals were never intended to be anything except personal thoughts and observations. ("They were my psychiatrist," she told me on the phone one day, "and a good friend.") That objectivity makes them all the more credible. Although they were never meant to speak for or to others, such chronicles, free of affectation and unrevised, often do.

Initially, I imagined Mary Alden sitting at a table, all her journals piled around her. As she read aloud entries from one decade after another, I, the light-handed editor sitting before her, would add quotations marks or italics, maybe a transition sentence or two, while the important words would be ones she wrote in her own hand. But I did not act on my instincts quickly enough, and now all her journals are locked away.

With the stipulation that her donations remain confidential for a hundred years, Mary Alden presented her private papers, which included photographs, letters, and her journals, to the South Carolina Department of Archives and History.

But she doesn't really need those prompts. She pulls anecdotes from her long, remarkable life the way a magician draws a silk scarf from his sleeve. The times of her life remain fixed in her memory, and, in a blink, she can conjure Hagood, the place where she grew up. There, her mother's family faced the challenges of keeping old plantation lands productive.

Henry III characterizes their Sumter County family as "land poor"—big acreage without the corresponding revenue.

In the Deep South's Depression years, tenant farmers, sharecroppers and proprietors all endeavored to stay afloat. Many events changed the region, but the land remained the same, hard to work and slow to pay. Landowners hoped to make a living for themselves as well as those that relied upon them for their income. Mary Alden grew up in these lean times.

In the early years of her life, when the stove was a wood-burning one and the icebox was exactly that, the kitchen belonged entirely to the cook and the family dressed for dinner. The children had a nursemaid. Help cleaned the house and tended the yard and labored in the fields while maiden aunts gathered the whole lot, relatives and workhands alike, for morning prayers.

Like their mother before them, Mary Alden and her brother, Jim, were reared with the daily business of a large farm whirring around them. Their prayer-leading aunts, and later an uncle and another aunt, owned Ellerbe's Mill, a place of commerce and the epicenter of social interaction.

Built around 1830, the three-story complex's top floor was equipped with a cotton gin and a sawmill while the lower floors housed the corn mill. Nobody had cash then, and the toll for grinding—one-tenth—was measured by a coffee can.

Before the backdrop of farm and mill, busy store and domestic bustle, Mary Alden rode on a school bus that forded Rafting Creek on its route to and from Hillcrest School. There, she and her brother earned the grades to win academic scholarships. Mary Alden would attend Coker College; Jim, The Citadel.

"Mother graduated high school at the end of the Great Depression, during the early war years when cotton and grain prices were just recovering from historic lows," explained Henry III. "To rural Sumter County families, black and white, their focus boiled down to one of survival. In that, the Ellerbe's Mill community may have been typical. From oldest to youngest, every soul made his or her contribution. Together they suffered, and together they survived."

The Ellerbe's Mill store granted credit and the corn grinding mill provided jobs; gardens grew and owners shared, teenagers did yard work. A cooperative culture rose out of this struggle. Henry cited the ritual of hog killing and sausage-making as a good example of how the society worked. On a cold winter day, families would assemble to do their part, and for their efforts, each received a cut of meat.

HENRY AND MARY ALDEN, 1942

Mary Alden may have missed the familiarity of home but she was ready to expand her horizons at college. She soon met Henry, Jr., and he called on her whenever he could. They enjoyed dates in the front parlor, the only kind of courting permissible.

"Coker was Baptist then and strict," Mary Alden pointed out. "But my mother went to

Confederate College in Charleston. In her day, they were told nice girls didn't look out the windows."

In 1942, Mary Alden's classmates elected her "Beauty Queen," and after all the girls put photographs of their boyfriends on the wall, Henry won the vote for favorite college sweetheart.

Out for a steak and dancing at Gus Ward's, the place to be in Camden in the 40's, she and Henry must have made a striking couple. But when World War II broke out in the middle of their romance, Henry volunteered for the Navy as a "90-day wonder" (OCS).

"He wrote to me every day," said Mary Alden. "He proposed to me in a letter and he sent a ring. Can you imagine, sending a ring through the mail?" Mary Alden shook her head, still surprised as she thought of it.

She saved Henry's letters, donating those as well to the archives. Many arrived with holes where censors cut out words and lines considered to give away too much. She also kept the difficult to read V-mails, photographs taken of servicemen's original letters and sent by the government on miniature postcards.

On October 15, 1942 Henry was Gunnery Officer aboard a destroyer, the USS Meredith, on a mission to resupply the marines on Guadalcanal when it came under attack by thirty-eight Japanese bombers and torpedo planes. The destroyer took multiple hits and broke into three pieces before it sank. For three days and nights the surviving crew and officers clung to life rafts and literally fought off sharks. The scene was gruesome. Between the bombs and torpedoes and frenzied sharks, only 81 men survived out of the original 273 on board.

When Henry came home on recuperative leave, he and Mary Alden decided they wouldn't wait any longer to marry. Due to gas rationing, no one could be expected in January of '43 to drive to a church and then to a reception, so both ceremony and celebration took place at Millvale, home of Mary Alden's uncle and aunt, Perry and Mary Brown. Even so, the two hundred or so guests had to receive special dispensation from the Office of Price Administration to attend, a fact that made headlines in the Sumter newspaper.

Henry Carrison, Sr. arranged for the couple's honeymoon through Camden's old Kirkwood Hotel. The newlyweds boarded a troop train to get to their destination.

"On a troop train, it was bad as it could be," said Mary Alden. "Crowded and rough. And troops had to be fed first. I took aspirin the

Millvale has changed little since it was built in 1890.

Millvale Plantation

whole way and Henry drank bourbon. We were going to Florida, and I saw our stop coming, but Henry said, 'No, we have a little ways to go,'

Washington County Public Library
1444 Jackson Avenue
Chipley, FL 32428

and so on we rode. He was wrong and I was right, but I didn't hold it over him. Finally, we got back to our hotel only to find it was an old people's retirement hotel, and here we were, married just one day! They looked at us like we were freaks."

Someone pitied the couple and loaned them bikes. Pedaling around and about Palm Beach, they happened upon a deserted shore. Mary Alden, in a stylish two-piece bathing suit, and Henry decided to stop and enjoy the sun. By and by, still unable to get over having such a beautiful spot to themselves, they went for a dip.

"I soon found out why nobody else was there," said Mary Alden. "A Portuguese Man-o'-War wrapped itself right around me. He dug in his tentacles exactly where my middle lay bare. Henry was wild trying to get them off and the pain of those stings, it was just terrible. Oh, how I wished then I'd had been wearing a one-piece."

For two years after they married, the Navy stationed Henry in Norfolk. When he went back to sea, Mary Alden returned to Magnolia Hall in Hagood, to her mother, Susan, and her widowed grandfather, Dr. Marion Singleton Kirk. Many things seemed the same. The fields still needed working and there was still a line at the mill. Emma Gardner helped with little Henry, just as she would help with Kirk, Susan and Perry when they came along.

Now a young mother, Mary Alden fell back into the arms of her extended family and into the familiar rhythm of home. She attended the Church of Ascension, founded by her great aunt, Ellen Ellerbe. She read, and she wrote in her journal.

Once the war was over, Henry joined her in Hagood. He and Mary Alden's Uncle Perry combined forces at the mill. In addition to grinding the famers' corn, they started buying corn in bulk. Henry successfully took on the expansion of their business, and throughout the fifties, when cornbread was still a Southern staple, grocery stores in Sumter, Camden and Columbia proudly advertised Browns' or Brown and Carrison Meal. Henry and his amiable crew of helpers did everything from loading the trucks to bagging and delivery.

"Those days," said Henry III, "were a lot of fun, with everybody pitching in." The business might have been expanded further, he surmised, but government regulations and the age of the mill dissuaded the partners.

"The wooden building was old and 19th Century equipment like belting and granite wasn't designed for mass production any more than using water power was when diesel was available," he said.

The eventual shutting down of the mill signified the end of an era for the family and the vicinity. All around the South, the old world and the old ways were dying.

"It was different then, when I was growing up and when I was raising my family," acknowledged Mary Alden. "It was an innocent time. I can't think of how to explain it, but I know this: I loved the people that worked for us and with us, and I know that they loved me."

Hard times: that's one explanation of what united them, but perseverance united them as well as tribulation.

Although Mary Alden must have written a sad note on the occasion of the mill's closing, she had the garden and her family to consider, piano lessons to teach. Although she admitted that when she married, she "couldn't even boil water," she would be honing her culinary skills. In time, condiments – pickles, relishes, conserves, chutneys, and jellies—would become her specialties. And the Church of the Ascension was going to require an organist, a need she would fill for thirty-two years. Eventually, she would serve as a senior warden.

As one chapter ended, another began, then one more and another, until the number of Mary Alden's journals grew great enough to take up a good-sized shelf. Surely she made notes about her garden—the exotic night-blooming cereus or angel trumpet, flowering in her yard as if were meant to grow there—or about fishing, about the weather or the news of the day or just the news of *her* day.

Somewhere in one of her journals, she might have written how, when she was out frog-gigging, a big bass leapt up towards the spotlight that she was holding and collided with her face. A week later she still had a black eye. She probably wrote about her four children, as they grew and scattered and began lives of their own. She must have recorded her grief, the deaths of the generation before, that of her daughter, Susan, and her husband, Henry. She must have written about her fading vision, too, and considered what to do about it.

Mary Alden, country born and bred, decided to move to town.

She proceeded to remodel a historic cottage and, of course, she landscaped the yard. Just outside her bedroom window on Lyttleton Street, she planted a six-by-eight foot wading pool in papyrus and water lilies. She bought goldfish, although Henry III argued against them.

He expected her brightly colored fish would fall prey to a heron or a kingfisher. "These might do well in Japan or China, but not in South Carolina," he told her. "Here our fish don't advertise."

Two weeks later, Henry wasn't surprised when she told him some of her fish had gone missing.

"But Mother's never been afraid to take a stand, even in the face of logic and reason," he said. "Nothing I could say would convince her that the culprit was probably a bird that fished for a living and for whom minnows were a routine breakfast."

'Coons were to blame, Mary Alden insisted.

"I paid a pretty price for those goldfish, and I'll be damned if I'm going to just stand by and watch them disappear," she informed her son.

Henry maintained that raccoons wouldn't waste their time on two-inch minnows, but Mary Alden bought a Hav-a-Heart wire trap anyway. That night, she baited it with crunchy peanut butter and set it by the pool.

"The next morning, she checked outside her window," said Henry. "Sure enough, there was a big male raccoon pacing and snarling in the trap."

Over the next six months, Mary Alden caught a total of 18 raccoons plus a 'possum and two house cats.

I hope she wrote that story down in her journal.

I hope that the pages of them are filled back to front with her meditations and her magic, her sense of delight.

A hundred years from now, when someone like me, or someone like you, comes across them, I hope her words come alive and the reader can see how one life, in a particular time and place, was observed, put on paper, lived in full.

Quiet Lives
Douglas Wyant

> *Make it your ambition to lead a quiet life.*
> 1 Thessalonians 4:11

Friday, July 12, 1946: *We were married at 6:00 o'clock by Rev. W.R. Pettigrew. Ate at Francis Marion Hotel.*

The bride, Wilma Bradley—a sharecropper's daughter from Cassatt, South Carolina—had graduated from Midway High School in 1940. Unable to find work locally, she and her sister Alma were hired as nurse's aides at Eastern State Hospital in Williamsburg, Virginia, in 1942, through the intercession of a cousin whose husband was stationed at Fort Eustis near Newport News.

The new aides were assigned to a women's ward in the mental health facility. Once, one of the patients, who had worked as a beautician, offered to give Wilma a haircut. At the time, no one objected, but when she told this story in old age, Mother questioned her own sanity, although she admitted she was well pleased with her new look.

In hopes of better hours, the sisters left the hospital to wait tables at the Ironbound Inn in Williamsburg. Since no one had much money, tips were small, but they enjoyed the attention of young servicemen stationed at Richmond or Norfolk.

Another waitress suggested they move to Florida. But Alma didn't like Florida at all, so they only stayed two weeks. On the way back to promised jobs in Williamsburg, the sisters stopped in Charleston, where they both met their future husbands while working as waitresses in a King Street restaurant.

The groom, Elbert Wyant, was a sailor who hailed from the landlocked state of West Virginia. On October 3, 1938, two months shy of his seventeenth birthday, he had enrolled in the Civilian Conservation Corps. While stationed at Camp F-18 at Neola, West Virginia, he hauled crushed rock and gravel in a 2-ton dump truck and men and material in a 1½-ton stake truck, driving a total of 2,132 miles without an accident. But he worked primarily as a blacksmith until his honorable discharge on September 23, 1940.

He enlisted in the U.S. Navy May 24, 1941, in Bluefield, West Virginia. After boot camp at Norfolk, Virginia, he was assigned to the *USS Bowditch*, a surveying ship, on which he served throughout World War II in the South Pacific. By the end of the war, he had been promoted to Motor Machinist Mate First Class. After a brief stint at Parris Island, he was transferred to the naval yard at Charleston, South Carolina. One fine day in 1946, he and some of his shipmates breezed into a restaurant on King Street.

Both were born in December 1921—Elbert on the 13th; Wilma on the 30th—but she refused to believe him until he showed her his driver's license. He was so lively she thought he was much younger. And he was short—only five-five. In a photograph taken with two buddies, he stood between them, beneath their outstretched arms.

Although barely five-four in stocking feet, Wilma was taller than he when she wore heels. His family always called him by his given name, but everyone else called him *Shorty*.

On a trip in October 1947 from South Carolina to West Virginia, to show off his new bride to his parents, grandparents, brothers, sisters, aunts, uncles, cousins, and neighbors, Shorty listed their expenses in a spiral-bound, pocket notebook: taxi, $1.00, two bus tickets, $27.07, breakfast for two, 82¢, dinner, $1.30, and supper, $1.69. When they arrived in Hinton at 10 a.m., after a long tiresome trip, they got cleaned up in a hotel room, $3.47. At 2 p.m., they caught the bus, $1.20, for the eighteen-mile trip to Shorty's home. They were either too anxious or too excited to eat breakfast or lunch. Shorty only spent 11¢ for coffee that morning and 14¢ for Coke that afternoon.

When they returned to Charleston on the fourth of November, after stopping to visit Wilma's family in Camden, they had a terrible time finding an apartment. And, at $10.00 per week, the rent was two dollars more than their previous place.

Numbers were important to my parents. They kept records of hours worked and bills paid. In their careful accounting of time and money, I like to think that they were only following the example of our Creator who numbers the hairs on our heads.

In June 1947—after his discharge from active duty in Charleston in April and my birth in Camden in May—Daddy, Mother, and I moved into a small clapboard house, which rented for $15.00 a month, on a narrow strip of land between Highway 20 and Lick Creek in Green Sulphur Springs, West Virginia, a mile south of Daddy's childhood home. Although water from nearby springs stank like rotten eggs, cattle often waded through the creek to drink the sulfur water.

Like their neighbors, they had no indoor plumbing, so their initial purchases included a tub, $1.50, bucket and dipper, 65¢, in addition to a set of dishes, $8.77, mixing bowls, $3.03, mixing spoon, $1.04, tea kettle, $1.98, strainer, 15¢, sheets, $1.85, shades, $3.88, clothes pins, 15¢, broom, 91¢, mop, $1.30, hoe, $1.00, chicken feed, $1.64, chicken wire, $1.50, and groceries, $6.18.

Unable to find a steady job—despite frequent trips to Hinton and Rainelle and occasional trips to Rupert and Belick Knob—Daddy collected twenty dollars a week in unemployment compensation. He supplemented the meager government stipend with work as a day laborer for Lewis Withrow and Earl Hicks. He harvested corn. Cut fence posts. Mowed and thrashed buckwheat. Cut and stacked hay. Dug Irish potatoes. Gathered pumpkins. Plowed fields. Planted winter wheat. Shucked and shelled ears of corn. Helped his father operate a grist mill. Butchered hogs. And lent Basil Blakenship a hand when he put a roof on an outbuilding.

He also plowed, planted, and hoed his own garden. Picked blackberries and cherries. Raised chickens and a hog. And hunted often—killing squirrels, groundhogs, rabbits, and pheasant—not for sport, but for sustenance.

Working together during the summer of 1947, Mother and Daddy canned eighteen quarts of cherries, twenty-six quarts of blackberries, fifteen quarts of peaches, ten quarts of beets, thirty-three quarts of string beans, seventeen quarts of tomatoes, five quarts of okra and tomatoes, and three quarts of corn. They also prepared seventeen pints of cherry preserves, six pints of peach jelly, twelve pints of blackberry jelly, sixteen pints of blackberry jam, and three quarts of peach butter.

On Tuesday, April 13, 1948, while Mother washed clothes, Daddy drove to a coal mine, looking for work. All he got was promises.

The next day, while Mother ironed clothes, Daddy returned to the mine. The foreman told him to come back Monday.

Monday, the foreman told Daddy to come back Wednesday.

Wednesday, the foreman told Daddy to come back Thursday.

Thursday, Daddy finally went to work for Bowyer & McClintic, a company that operated a strip mine at Spring Dale, eight miles north of Green Sulphur Springs. He returned home sore and tired and covered with coal dust.

One of the most frequent diary entries in 1948 is *Shorty worked 10 hours*. But work at the mine the following years was sporadic, delayed by bad weather, defective machinery, or disputes between the union and the mine owners. In addition to taxes, the company withheld two dollars in union dues and two-fifty for a burial fund each pay period.

On Friday, February 11, 1949, *We borrowed fifteen hundred dollars from the bank*, the National Bank of Summers in Hinton, to purchase the Tincher place, a fifty-acre farm near the unincorporated community of Elton, two miles north of Green Sulphur Springs and a mile off the highway. Over the next week, his grandfather and his brother Cecil helped Daddy hang sheetrock and made minor repairs in the old farmhouse. Although we moved into the house in the middle of February, we used a coal-oil lamp after dark until the house was wired and a power line was strung up the mountain. On Monday, May 23, 1949, Mother noted, *A Man from Electric Power Co. connected the wires. Sure was glad.*

As a young married couple, my parents enjoyed simple pleasures—a sleigh ride in February, a watermelon in July, roasted marshmallows in August, cake and ice cream on birthdays. They went window-shopping, took rides in the country, and shared meals with family and friends. Mother kept a record of who they visited and who visited them each week.

In the diary that she kept the first four years of their marriage, Mother only mentioned going to church once, while on a brief visit to her family. But after Daddy's conversion, when he was about 30, we became active members of the Elton Community Church.

When we moved to Camden, we became faithful members of Beaverdam Baptist, a small country church near Cassatt that Mother had attended as a child. We were one of those families who were there every time the doors opened: Sunday mornings, Sunday and Wednesday evenings. In addition to singing in the choir, Daddy served as a deacon and Sunday school superintendent. Church services were so much a part of our lives that not attending due to inclement weather was noted on a pocket calendar Mother kept in 1968.

Mother only had four, four-inch lines on which to record the most important events of her day. All her diary entries were short and simple:

Walked down town. Went to a movie, "A Song of Old Montana." Ate supper at Palm Bay.

Spent a quiet evening at home. Listened to the radio. Washed each other's hair.

Shorty worked 8 hours. I baked a coconut cake.

Occasionally, the only entry in her diary was *Usual day.* Perhaps there came a time when the events of her life seemed too mundane to mention. Or else she just didn't have the time or the energy or the desire to describe her days.

The last entry in her diary is dated Sunday, September 3, 1950: *Cecil & Aaron ate dinner with us. Wayne and Douglas both are feeling bad. We rode up to where Shorty works in the Jeep.* The previous day he had traded the 1941 Chevrolet he had purchased in 1947 for a 1950 Willys, the only new vehicle he would ever own.

After work petered out at the mine, Daddy found part-time work at a filling station. He was only paid for work done, earning a dollar to fix a flat or grease a car. From April until December 1954, he tallied up his pay each month in a grease-stained pocket notebook. Seven days in April he wrote *NONE*. His total income for April was $86.75. By July, he was desperate enough to seek work in South Carolina.

In a letter postmarked JUL 21 1954 ELTON W. VA. addressed to Elbert Wyant c/o Sam Bradley in Camden, S.C., Mother wrote, *Have you found a job yet? I don't know what we are going to do if you don't soon find something. We got a letter from the bank. They said our payment was past due. The kids ask me every day if we got a letter from Daddy. If you don't have a job and can't find one and don't have a promise of one, you might as well come on back, if you have the money.*

That fall, back in West Virginia, he supplemented his income as a mechanic with farm labor. He disked fields, hauled corn and coal and wood, shucked corn, and operated a grist mill. But he still wasn't able to earn enough to meet his monthly obligations.

In December 1954, Daddy borrowed a dump truck and moved our furniture into a rented house in Camden. He worked briefly for Jaclyn Hosiery Mill, Rainwater Furniture Company, and as co-owner of W&W Variety Store. He distributed Rawleigh products and pumped gas for Hess Oil. Before opening his own garage in 1966, he worked as a mechanic for DeKalb Motors.

Mother was the first one to get up in the morning and the last one to go to bed at night. Never idle, she washed and ironed clothes, mopped floors, cooked meals, raised three children, and worked at a variety of jobs: behind the lunch counter at Walgreen's Drug Store on South Broad Street, at the Greyhound bus station on DeKalb Street, then in Skyline Manufacturing Company's cafeteria. At 62, she retired from Tic Tac Company as a bundler in the sewing plant that made children's clothes.

In 1996, when they announced their fiftieth wedding anniversary in the *Chronicle-Independent*, Daddy and Mother selected a photograph a friend had taken Sunday, July 21, 1946, on the South Battery in Charleston.

Daddy continued to work until he was 75, in his garden as well as in his garage, in obedience to the command of the apostle to *work*

with your own hands so that you will be respected by everyone and not dependent on anyone. After surviving open-heart surgery, he succumbed to cancer in June 1997.

Mother died in December 2009, fifteen days before her eighty-eighth birthday. Her obituary summed up her entire life in one generic sentence: *She loved her family and enjoyed cooking for them.*

I keep a sprawling, haphazard, loose-leaf notebook. On January 29, 2010—just over a month after Mother's death—I paraphrased a sentence I lifted from *A Free Life*, a novel by Ha Jin: *A good life should be uneventful, filled with small delights, each appreciated and enjoyed like a gift.*

The Left-Handed Tomato Thrower
Bobbi Adams

Black and white photographs we have of my grandmother Adams show her to be short, stocky, and swarthy. I don't remember any of this, of course, but I do remember she kept chickens. Standing over the black coal-burning stove, Ma extracted golden yolks from the hens after they were killed for meat. Her home had neither heat nor air conditioning. The kitchen was the center of the house. (There, she kept the dish of homemade candy, which came from the local pharmacy, that I remember so well. I would know the taste immediately if I ever found it again.)

The yolks of the eggs were bright yellow. After all, these were free-range chickens. Every night she called the hens into the chicken coop. There, in quiet, with the hens free from fear of the weasels and foxes that played in the pastures, golden eggs appeared.

Ma collected eggs every day. I helped her with that when I visited as a three-year-old. I never remember being afraid of the hens or of being pecked. My father, "Pop," would take only me with him for visits. My other sisters were too young.

Ma kept roosters, too. The roosters kept the hens happy so they could lay those golden eggs. Pop used to take an ax and cut off the heads of the chickens, when they stopped laying eggs or when we needed them for dinner. The chickens used to run around the yard headless once they were killed. I remember Pop killing chickens this way at home, too, which was an hour's drive away.

I recently asked my three sisters if they remembered Ma at all. My second sister has very vague memories of her. My third sister, Kay, has none at all. Diana, the youngest, was exactly a year old to the day when Ma died in 1949. I was almost ten.

I remember my father showing me the graves of Ma's first four children in the Presbyterian Cemetery in Rockaway, New Jersey. There were no names or headstones. Against a fence lay four unnamed stillborn girls, four pregnancies in two years. I doubt they were anywhere near full term, but I do remember four graves. Ma carried these children long enough to be identified as female and then she lost them.

> There were no names or headstones. Against a fence lay four unnamed stillborn girls, four pregnancies in two years.

Her first living child was my Uncle Les born in 1900. Her second living child was my father, who was not breathing when he was born on Christmas Day in 1904. The midwife, Ma's mother, Granny, whom I vaguely remember in a four poster with a night cap on her head, would wait forty years after that for a girl to be born into the family. That was me.

My Uncle Les, Ma's first live child, was not named after his father. He enlisted in the Navy at age sixteen in WWI. Les quit school in the eighth grade. When he came home at the end of World War I, he married a cousin, once removed. Ma thought Uncle Lester should not marry. He did it anyway and had three sons, the youngest of whom was ten years older than me. Ma's second son, my father, was named Robert Adams, Jr. after his father. My grandfather Adams worked in the iron mines of Hibernia, New Jersey. "A very good miner," he held the job of mine foreman in the iron mines of northern New Jersey. He died from brown lung in 1927.

Ma was removed from school when she was in the second grade. To increase the family income, she washed miner's clothes and made Cornish pasties. These were sold to the iron miners in Hibernia. Pop remembered this hearty dish from his childhood. Pasties, wrapped up in rags, stayed warm until noontime in the mines, when the men rested for lunch. In those days (early twentieth century) there were no unions. Miners were not allowed out of the mines to the surface to eat, rest, and breathe fresh air.

Pasties contained potatoes, meat, turnips or parsnips, carrots, and onions. Ma grew all those vegetables in her garden. I do not remember her growing flowers.

Here in Lee County, South Carolina, root crops are grown. In the fall I eat turnip and rutabaga roots as well as delicious sweet potatoes. Country folk here still have extremely large vegetable gardens. I am fortunate enough to have friends who share from these gardens.

I still make pasties from scratch when I am with my youngest sister, Diana. Even the pastry is prepared from scratch, although I no longer use lard to make the crust.

I also had Cornish pasties on my first visit to England. I left Bo, Sierra Leone, West Africa during school break. I was very ill that first year in Africa. Despite the prophylactic I took daily, the mosquitoes found me. I contracted malaria. I went to England to recover and tried to find my English roots but there is no record at Somerset House of my great-grandmother, who I knew as granny. Her name is variously recorded in church records as Mary Elizabeth and as Elizabeth Mary Sparnon. There are very few Sparnons registered in church records in Somerset House. It is thought the family might have been French Huguenots who escaped to England during one of the persecutions.

I went to Cornwall that first summer in England. It was beautiful. There were played out copper mines everywhere. Cornish miners emigrated to America from England when the mines failed. They got jobs in the iron mines of northern New Jersey. The New Jersey mines date back before the American Revolution. Pop gave me a cannon ball from the Revolution made from the iron in those mines. The cannonballs from these mines helped to win the American Revolution.

I recently passed the cannonball on to my great-nephew, along with the history written by Ma's brother, Fred Hanschka, the one who asserted that Robert Adams, Sr. was "a good miner."

Granny, my great-grandmother and the midwife for the miner's families, was a child in 1866, when the call came to board the ships at Penzance for America. She snatched a saltcellar from the table and put it into her pocket. That was the only memento she brought with her from England, or so the family story goes. My sister, Kay, still has it.

Ma was fiercely determined that neither of her sons would ever go into the mines. When the miners struck for better working conditions, she was out on the strike lines throwing ripe tomatoes from her garden at men armed with guns. The mining company hired strikebreakers, who used guns to shoot at anything that moved around the mines. They always wanted to know who that left-handed tomato thrower was according to my father. Ma almost lost one of her two sons then. Pop remembered being shot at as a young boy and the family dog, my dad's pet Jack Russell, was shot and killed.

> When the miners struck for better working conditions, she was out on the strike lines throwing ripe tomatoes from her garden at men armed with guns...They always wanted to know who that left-handed tomato thrower was according to my father.

All miners lived in mine owned houses and bought supplies on credit from the company stores. My father told me stories about what it was like when I was a child, and I saw the house he lived in.. After he retired, my father took me and my youngest sister to the site of the house. All that remained was the cellar hole.

I also realized in the seventies, when spending a prolonged visit to New Jersey, that both Granny and Ma were illiterate, but my Adams' great-grandparents were not. I remember Ma kept dogs, too. As a little girl, I remember a succession of male dogs in the pen behind the garage. Every dog I ever remember was named Rex, the Latin word for king. There was a succession of "Kings" penned up. I believe they were all collies.

Ma and Rex

Ironically, or perhaps not, my great-grandfather was Robert King Adams. He is supposed to have been the illegitimate child of a mainline Philadelphia family, the "Kings." This Robert fought in the Civil War for the north. Family tales say he had a saber cut across his shoulder. He died falling into a gristmill.

After Ma died, I borrowed Nancy, a female collie from neighbors. I used to walk her everywhere. Mother did not allow pets in the house. Four children to clean up after were enough for her.

The first dog mother allowed in the house was a collie named Lady. She arrived when I was in Africa. I have a picture of my father, dressed in Muslim garb I sent home for him, with Lady.

Whether dogs named "Rex" or "Kings" named Robert bear any relationship to one another I do not know, however, in my mind they are connected. I often wonder if the story about his birth was true.

My father, as long as he was able, put his head under the cold water spigot to wash his face in the morning. Ma's house had an outside pump and a three-holer. I believe there were twelve seniors in my father's high school graduating class. Pop also went off to college on scholarship at Ma's insistence. He majored in mathematics. Pop really wanted to be a railroad engineer, not a high school math teacher, principal and interim superintendent. He loved steam engines and used to walk us over to the train station in Fanwood, New Jersey, where I grew up so we could watch these huge machines pull up at the station, belching steam and smoke. We stood on the wooden trestle overpass and looked through the timbers as the trains passed beneath us.

In college in my parents' time, students were seated alphabetically, girls first. Since mother's last name was Whipple, Daddy was seated immediately behind her in class. And that is how they met at Alfred University. My mother was the daughter of a college trustee. On the maternal side, she was the fourth generation of women in her family to attend Alfred. I believe Content was first, then Amanda, then Eola and finally my mother, Georgeola.

I was grown and back from Africa before I travelled to Alfred. They have a famous carillon, but the thing I remember most about the visit in June for a college class reunion, was the family cemetery. The wildflowers were in bloom all over the gravesites, many of which were very old. I especially remember the scent of the lemon daylilies and the blue forget-me-nots in the grass. My sister Diana went with us, but was sick the day we visited the cemetery. Alfred is in the Snow Belt, so none of those wildflowers made it in my southern garden.

The year Pop graduated from Alfred University, Ma and her sister Edna, came to graduation. We have that picture of the two of them with Pop. How Ma managed to keep herself going during the depression that followed, I really don't know. Ma thought my father was too young to marry at twenty-four, but she did keep both of her sons out of the mines.

I also do not know when Ma married Cyrus Dixon Righter, but Pa, as I called him, is the grandfather I remember. He kept dairy cows. I loved the dairy barn as a child. This is where I watched weasels in the cow pasture and saw the chickens laying golden eggs. The farm was on the edge of a swamp. The road was dirt. The last time I visited, the road to the dairy was paved. It was called Righter Road and the dairy barn and house were still there in Succasunna, New Jersey. The pastures were gone, filled with new homes. No weasels and foxes any longer.

Ma and I used to walk down the dirt road to the swamp. Here we picked blueberries together. I made blueberry pie this summer using the same pastry recipe I use for Cornish pasties. Mother remembered summers on the farm when I was a year old. There are pictures of this. On a hot July day just before my first birthday in 1940, I learned to stand in the playpen. Up and down I went to the point of exhaustion. I was not exhausted, but mother and both grandmothers were exhausted watching me.

Thinking about the pastry, I still have to do this at Christmas for my youngest sister in Florida. I've given all three of my sisters the recipe, but they are too heavy handed. If you knead the pastry too much it gets tough. Mine always comes out just right.

Ma's legacy to me is more than memories. I have the garden tools she used. They were forged by her father, Billy Hanschka, who was the Hibernia Mine blacksmith. I have a shovel, a garden rake, a pitch fork and lots of pick axes. I used all of these tools when I hand dug my garden here, spading about five tons of moats from the local gin into the hard red clay of my back yard. It is no wonder my knees are replaced and my shoulders filled with bone spurs. From Ma, I also have cuttings grown from the Christmas cactus she brought into bloom in an unheated house. One has to put it  through "enforced" misery. Ma gave mother a piece of this cactus when she married my father.

Mother kept the plant going for forty years. It never bloomed once. It was not until a New Jersey master gardener told me to put the plant through enforced misery that we finally managed to get it to bloom. To do this we put the cactus on an unheated porch for a month, withholding water and fertilizer. It bloomed for my wedding.

Ma kept the cactus in a large barrel in an unheated house, which also had a dirt cellar Here the root crops she grew were kept cool during the winter and tomatoes and other vegetables she put up from her garden were stored. I still have the canning jars she used. In my kitchen, they store bulk teas, herbs from my garden such as ginger root and sage.

Ma also kept a pot of tea in an iron teakettle on her wood-burning stove. The tea was extremely strong by the end of the day, and in order to drink it, the dark liquid had to be strained through a sieve to remove the leaves. She always drank her tea with milk, a practice I still follow.

Two weeks on the Road
Kathryn Etters Lovatt

At 94, my father, Alexander Etters, is still so sharp, I am not his equal in the daily crossword. He keeps a catalogue of jokes right where he

ALEX ETTERS, 1939

can get to them, on the tip of his tongue, and he repeats them with triumph, delivering a perfect punch line every time. Each yarn he spins comes packed with his trademark wit.

"I've got a lot of stories," he says. "And some of them are *mostly* true."

What is completely true is that my father, born March 3, 1920 in Chester, was the eighth and last child, the seventh boy, of Sarah Letitia Sloane Miller Etters and Keistler Campbell Etters. Over his lifetime, Grandfather had worked his way up from sweeper to general manager in a string of textile mills.

"He wanted to retire early and become a gentleman farmer," Daddy remembers. "You know the definition of a gentleman farmer, don't you?" Although he wears his new and perfect teeth, when my father grins like this, I see the devilish gap between the old ones. "A gentleman farmer," he reminds me, "is a man who makes more money in town than he loses in the country."

Grandfather Etters tried farming in Chester, but my dad says he had no luck. "Boll weevils ate his cotton up, and then somebody or another convinced him that the Sandhills of Kershaw County got so hot during growing season, the weevils just fell off the plants and when they did, the ground below cooked them to death."

K.C. ETTERS FAMILY, 1921

My grandfather promptly purchased several tracts of land—some from Grover Welch, sheriff at the time, some from the Hortons, enough finally to accumulate about 800 acres. The farm sits 12 miles from Camden in the community of Boonetown, spelled with a pair of o's but pronounced as if there were only one.

Weevils would not fall off the plants and die, but Granddaddy didn't know that yet in 1926 when he commissioned George Creed to build a house that took nearly two years to complete. Heart pine logs for the floors were cut off the acres where a World War II airport would be erected in 1941. Cypress siding came out of the Okefenokee in Georgia and arrived by train in Dekalb.

"We put in a Delco System, the only way in the twenties to get electric power so far away from town," Daddy explains. "Some nights, people would come around and stare at the electric lights. You'd think we'd hung stars on the ceiling."

My father grew up there, on the land where we now seed pines instead of cotton. He rode mules and picked berries and learned to plow. He grew into a crack shot. He caught fish and cleaned them, skinned rabbits. He ate a lot of hickory nuts, too, or, as my father says, "hickernuts." His fondness for them would supply the moniker he carries to this day: *Hick*. He went to Baron DeKalb School, the old one on Highway 521 that, in the words of its alma mater, stands "on yon hill."

In 1933—"maybe '34," Daddy concedes—when he was 13, or 14, he worked a whopping ten days for the WPA. The Works Progress Administration was part of America's New Deal, an attempt to provide relief for the unemployed. Through the WPA, the government made region of the US, got the least money– certainly not enough to pave old country roads, but enough to top some of them off. Lockhart, a road that ran close by the Etters' house, was slated for such a resurfacing.

A field away from where Lewis Boone ran his store, a clay pit was scooped out and a stream of men showed up to excavate it.

The crew worked a stretch at a time, digging new pits when they hit chalk or if the hauling distance grew so far as to slow progress, whichever came first. They moved on then and cut a new hole nearer the next section of rough road. The running joke used to be that WPA stood for "We Piddle Around," but nobody piddled on this job, which hunched backs and stressed muscles.

"The long termers called themselves 'The Hoover Gang,'" says my father, "because even though the program was a Franklin Roosevelt inspiration, the Depression hit on Hoover's watch. Besides, *Hoover Gang*, I reckon they thought it had a better ring to it."

That year, with cold weather already set in and Christmas drawing near, extra help was needed. My dad and three of his brothers signed up.

Ninch, the oldest, went down in the pit with pick and shovel. Howard, K.C. and my father, all on holiday break from school, agreed to work as drivers. With them, they brought two of their father's wagons, which they had rigged so that the boards could be opened with the pull of a handle for dirt to fall through, and four twelve-hundred pound mules to pull them. Daddy remembers the names of those massive beasts: Roadie, January, Kit and Red.

"It was hard work for mules and men," he says. "Ten hours a day. The clay was wet and heavy and that winter was stinging cold." The one advantage the other brothers had over Ninch was that there were three drivers for two wagons. "Every third trip," says Daddy, "you got to back up to the fire."

The foreman's whistle signaled lunch, an hour breather that divided the day. When my father describes the men's lunch pails—old lard or golden syrup cans—hanging in the bare branches of trees, I imagine them as bright ornaments, strange silver fruits, on cowering limbs. The men reached up and pulled them down and took out whatever they had: cold biscuit and jelly, a piece of fried fatback, a sweet potato. As they ate, they squatted by the fire, trying to get warm.

"Me and my brothers ran home, not far down the road. We got to stay inside a little while, and Ma always had a pot of dried beans. We ate ourselves a helping. Ate whatever else she had to go with them."

Before the whistle sounded, they hurried back to their posts. Half of the day still lay ahead, half a day more of shoveling and running the wagon back and forth down Lockhart Road.

Although the work lasted only two frigid weeks, the brothers earned a small fortune. Ninch made 70 cents a day. The mules brought in $2.50 s day, as did the wagons; the drivers were considered part of the bargain.

For two weeks worth of labor, the Etters brothers earned a total of $57.00.

"All the farmers worried the WPA was going to ruin them," remembers Daddy. "The going rate for a hired hand was 35 cents a day and dinner. Ninch was doubling that."

My grandfather, who sat on the porch but owned the mules and wagons, would take money off the top, but once the brothers divided the rest, they came away with $13.00 apiece. When school started again, my father took his wages to show.

"Everyone wanted to have a look at it," he says, "because nobody could believe that much money actually existed."

What did he do with his fortune? Six dollars of it went toward a horse-blanket coat.

And what exactly is a horse blanket coat?

"A coat you couldn't find today," he replies, "and if you could, you couldn't afford to buy it."

Come spring, he sold the coat for $7.00 to his favorite brother, Howard, who wanted to wear it to The Carolina Cup. He was, my father says, the one among them "who always loved to dress up."

My father folds his arms over the hump of his belly, nods his head in self-approval. "I came out pretty good, I think, owning it all winter and then selling it for more than I paid in the first place. Howard wore that coat more times than I ever did anyhow. He was always wanting to borrow it, so I guess he thought he owed me the dollar profit."

The rest of his wages, he spent "a dime at a time."

"You get a lot of friends when you get a lot of money," he says, sporting that wide grin again. "Me and my friends, we enjoyed it till it was gone." He falls back into the soft nest of his chair, shrugs. "Better to live rich than die rich, that's what I say."

STILL ROCKIN' AT 94

TIES THAT BIND

Walking, I am listening to a deeper way. Suddenly all my
ancestors are behind me. Be still, they say. Watch and listen.
You are the result of the love of thousands.

Linda Hogan

Ties That Bind
Mindy Blakely

"Whose are you?" The bald man in the pin-stripped suit asked as if he actually believed some random kid would arrive in the middle of no-where Kingstree, South Carolina, for the sole purpose of crashing this party. Standing in the crowded front room of Aunt Sarah Beth's tiny blue house, I knew the correct response to this question.

"I'm Logan Junior's," I replied, shuffling my feet on the red carpet. Aunt Sarah Beth isn't really my aunt. In fact, I never figured out whose aunt she was because everyone called her by the same title.

"Oh, then you must be Jill," he said.

"No, Jill is my older sister." I pulled my hair behind my ears. Some of the adults on the other side of room cackled at a joke. My older brother Randy laughed along with that group.

"Then you must be Hopey." He smiled.

"No, Hope is my younger sister. I'm Mindy, the third child," I said.

"My goodness, I didn't realize Logan Junior had so many children. How many of you are there?" He wiped his nose on a tissue.

"Four." I answered. *Where was my cousin Nikki?*

"Goodness gracious. Well it's nice to see you," he patted me on the back and moved on to torture someone else.

I headed to the toilet, but of course someone else occupied it. SB's house consisted of three large rooms and only one restroom. A narrow archway separated the facilities on the left side of the inner room from the white cloth covered tables arranged in a semi-circle on the right side. I could see the bathroom door from my position across the dining area as I examined the platters full of goodies.

A large chocolate frosted cake displayed in the very center of the three tables tempted me. I *would* eat a piece of it this year. Finally the potty freed up, but it didn't contain enough paper towels to clean my legs from all the bean juice that had dribbled on me during the drive from Camden. Riding on the hump seat of Daddy's old brown Plymouth meant wearing spillage for the rest of the day, especially the way Daddy drove. I should have known better than to wear shorts in spite of the warm, breezy temperature on this August afternoon.

My mother didn't own any Tupperware, but she felt obligated to bring a dish every year which usually meant plastic containers covered with aluminum foil. After spending over two hours in the car if we weren't baptized in bean juice by the time we arrived, we would be drenched in corn sauce, or sweet tea, or watermelon slosh. Nothing beat feeling sticky all over and having everyone think you had peed in your pants.

"Mindy, hey, let's go outside," said my cousin Rhonda. We walked outside to the giant cornfield surrounding the house. Ever the tomboy, Rhonda ran to the lone tree in the front yard and proceeded to climb its only limb. Dust and sand blew up in our faces as a motorcycle gang flew by.

"Yay, the boys are here," Rhonda said, clamoring down to run after them. Yep, the male cousins had arrived. They hugged Rhonda. Me, they didn't know.

"Anyone up to go for a ride?" said Jack. Rhonda could not resist, but I didn't see the point of taking a motorcycle ride with my cousin. If it had been someone unrelated to me, like a boyfriend, maybe I would have reconsidered. After Rhonda left with Jack, the conversation instantly died. *What could I say to these redneck boys? Were they really my cousins? Why did they all look so dirty and scruffy? When would Nikki get here?*

Next the boys wanted to start up a softball game. *Yuck.* Finally Nikki swept outside looking like a fashion plate in her purple wrap around skirt and matching headband. She wore brown leather cowboy boots. Everyone gravitated toward her, especially the boys. She conversed so easily with them. I reminded myself that all of my cousins grew up and went to school together though. They knew each other inside and out. No secrets unshared between them. We were the outsiders who lived in a different town.

After greeting everyone, Nikki drew me aside to talk and make fun of the others. She and I liked more girly activities and soon found ourselves giggling over nothing. We always found fun things to do like viewing old photo albums or talking about boys and dating. I *so* wanted to be like her. Everything she did seemed cool in my eyes.

On my second trip past the food tables, I overheard my Aunt Frances and my Aunt Lois talking.

"Well I can't believe she moved in with her boyfriend, just like that!" said Frances. "What does her mother think?"

I pretended to examine the corn on the cob, potato salad, and yams. The aromas of baked ham, pecan pie, green bean casserole, and macaroni and cheese assaulted my senses.

"She was really too upset to come today, but Harold is just beside himself. He doesn't know what to do with her anymore," said Lois. I nearly choked on the chocolate chip cookie I had just inhaled from the dessert table. Harold was Nikki's father. She and I, both fourteen, would start high school in September.

"I declare," said Frances, "Has Harold thought about trying that tough love approach? I've been reading about it in some of the self-help books I enjoy so much and it sounds crazy, but they say it can really turn some kids around."

Lois grabbed hold of Frances's shoulder. "Listen, Frances, he has tried spankings, restrictions, tough love, and everything you can think of, but she's refuses to cooperate."

Frances shook her head, muttering, "umm, umm, umm."

"He's a good father and he loves that girl to pieces! He wouldn't let anything hurt her for all the world, but she's a teenager and convinced that she knows it all. She's hell bent determined to do what she wants to do. She's not a lunatic so you can't lock her up, but what is a parent supposed to do? I've just been praying every day that she will come to her senses and stops living in sin," said Lois.

"I will pray too," said Frances, "and I'm sure everything will work out all right. You call me if you need to talk. I mean it Lois, day or night. "

Lois, Nikki's grandmother, sniffled on a sob. I slipped into the loo to think. I didn't mean to eavesdrop. Should I talk to Nikki about it? If I did, she would know that the other family members were talking about her. I didn't want to hurt her feelings and I also didn't want her to sin. *What could Nikki be thinking? Why did she want to do this?* I know she had no idea how tormented her parents felt. I could not even imagine discussing such a decision with my own father. Daddy would kill me if Mama didn't beat him to the punch. Either way I'd be dead. End of story.

While I didn't agree with Nikki's decision, I still admired her for standing up to her parents over something she believed in. The devil in me knew I could never stand up to my parents that way, but she took more risks. I hoped she didn't end up pregnant or worse with some weird sexual disease. Kids our age shouldn't have to change diapers or race after screaming toddlers. Our best years were ahead of us.

Finally the coward inside decided it best for me to hold my silence about the whole matter. I said a prayer for her and went back outside. In my heart I believed she would eventually make the right decision, but I would continue to pray for her. We resumed our conversation while I pretended nothing had changed at all.

The adults finally stepped outside to tell us to come in and eat, but only after they had already served themselves. As usual, not one crumb of the chocolate cake had been left for us. Deep In my heart, I vowed to change that next time. With our sagging paper plates, we headed outside to the "kids' table." The kid's table was much smaller, about the size of a card table, and had child sized chairs also. The aromas of fried chicken and fresh watermelon sent swarms of flies and mosquitos over. Bringing relief from the summer heat, cold iced tea slid down our throats as we battled the insects for our meal. I could hear the boys at the other end of the table laughing about Jack and my sister Jill in relation to the nursery rhyme. I guess they wanted to create some lame humor. I sighed as I bit into a warm buttered roll.

With a group of boys, inevitably a food fight followed with chunks of potato salad and mashed potatoes flying off spoons at each other and soon at the rest of us. Laughter abounded and when the energy had been spent to finish eating and cleaning the mess, the boys raced off to continue their earlier softball game.

About an hour or so after the meal, the adults prepared to leave. Nikki and I exchanged addresses and promised to write each other, but we never did. As we headed to the car, Aunt Sarah Beth hollered, "Y'all come back real soon, hyar." Hyar is a one syllable word the Blakely family created to abbreviate the words "ye hear". Only a true Southerner could understand.

When we climbed into the car and resumed our previous positions, which meant the hump seat for me, my sister Hope said, "Daddy, if we get back early enough, can I go over to Tiffany's house for a little while?"

"No," Daddy said. "We will be home late and I don't want you kids running around the neighborhood after dark. Lots of dangerous people prowl around on weekend nights and you need your rest for school tomorrow."

As we drove home and I pondered our day at the Blakely family blowout, I realized how lucky I had been growing up and being disciplined in a Christian home. The rules kept us grounded. The Blakelys, in spite of all their faults, had always been religious and though Logan Jr. used to drag us kicking and screaming to this ritualistic festivity, I sensed the relatives really cared and I'd had more fun than I had expected. Soon teenage activities would get in the way and I would have even less desire to attend this annual event. I took comfort knowing that even if I never attended another Blakely family gathering, I'd still see them again someday. It will be a reunion no one wants to miss. When I stand outside those pearly gates, I have no doubt in my mind how I will respond to the question, "Whose are you?"

Unfortunately I do not have a family recipe for Chocolate Cake as I never learned who made the one at our reunions, but here is a simple recipe that I really like and I hope you will enjoy it as well.

Hershey's Perfectly Perfect Chocolate Cake

Ingredients:

2 cups sugar
1 3/4 cups all purpose flour
3/4 cups Hershey's cocoa
1 1/2 teaspoon baking powder
1 1/2 teaspoon baking soda
1 teaspoon salt
2 eggs
1 cup milk
1/2 cup vegetable oil
2 teaspoons vanilla extract
1 cup boiling water

Instructions:

Heat oven to 350 degrees F.
Grease and flour two nine inch baking pans.
Combine dry ingredients in large bowl.
Add eggs, milk, oil, and vanilla; beat on medium speed for two minutes
Stir in boiling water (batter will be thin)
Pour into pans. Bake for 30 to 35 minutes or until a wooden pick inserted in center comes out clean.
Cool for ten minutes. Remove from pans to wire racks.
Cool completely. Frost.
Makes 10 to 12 servings.

Perfectly Chocolate Chocolate Frosting

Ingredients:

1 stick (1/2 Cup) butter or margarine
2/3 cups Hershey's cocoa
3 cups powdered sugar
1/3 cup milk
1 teaspoon vanilla extract

Instructions:

> *Melt butter. Stir in cocoa. Alternately add powdered sugar and milk, beating on medium speed for two minutes or until it reaches spreading consistency.*
> *Add more milk if needed. Stir in vanilla.*
> *Makes about 2 cups.*

The Corner of Union and Fair
Jayne Padgett Bowers

"If Daddy hadn't died, I never would have gone into nurses' training," she said. And then by way of explanation, "He wouldn't have let me leave home, you know."

But leave home she did. Edna had been studying nursing in New Orleans, and in 1945, she arrived in Camden to complete her training. The young student lived in the nurses' dormitory on the corner of Union and Mill Streets, directly behind what was then called the Camden Hospital. Clad in their professional attire, she and her friends were frequently spotted trekking back and forth between the two buildings.

One day as she and a gaggle of young women were crossing to the hospital, Edna was noticed by a handsome young man, recently returned from Europe after serving in WWII. He was dating a friend of hers from "back home," but when Edward noticed this blue-eyed beauty with soft brown hair, he asked, "Who's that?"

"That's my friend, Edna Farmer," his date said.

Later, Ms. Farmer learned that the dashing chap had asked about her several times and from a variety of people. Trying to get a true picture of personality and character, he wanted to know whether she smoked or drank and whether she had a boyfriend. Still, he didn't ask her out. Was he shy? Not that interested?

In December of 1945, Edward and Edna became better acquainted. Suffering from kidney stones, Edward was admitted to Camden Hospital and had a private room on the second floor. In those days, patients spent more time convalescing in hospitals, and he was there for five days, thus giving the young couple a chance to observe each other and to chat on occasion.

At that time, young nurses bathed the older male patients, and the older nurses bathed the younger ones. Since she wasn't his nurse, Edna had no reason to go into Edward's room. A circumspect rule follower, she stayed away from the dark-haired patient despite his entreaties for a back massage.

Edna worked the night shift, and one night Edward rang the bell for assistance over and over again.

"I don't mean he rang it once and then waited a few minutes before ringing it again. I mean it was constant. Ring, ring, ring. I went in to see what he wanted, and he said he wanted a back rub. I told him I wasn't allowed to do that while I was on duty."

"Well, how about when you get off duty at 11?" he persisted.

"I'll do it if you'll stop ringing that bell. It's annoying," she said.

"He could really turn on the personality," she reminisced. "Once when I was taking his pulse, he smiled up at me and said, "I'm going to date you when I get out of here.""

Edward began to flirt in earnest, and one night as she and her friends were leaving the floor, they heard a distinct wolf whistle. Edna knew it was coming from the room near the staircase and said, "Oh, that's Edward. I told him I'd come by and speak to him before I left."

And speak she did…from the door. She was following rules, and besides, she couldn't figure this man out. Was he just flirting with her because of his boredom, or was he genuinely interested?

One evening Edna was asked to take Edward his food tray. At that time, the trays came up on a dumbwaiter, and the nurses finished the tray preparations in the diet kitchen. After getting his tray ready, she walked next door to his room. Already feeling a little nervous, she was even more ill at ease when she walked into his room and saw Edward sitting up in bed, his Aunt Carrie seated in a chair beside the bed.

Although they were chatting when Edna entered the room, the conversation stopped when she crossed the threshold, and they both grinned at her "from ear to ear." Why? What was going on? Had they been talking about her? Was Aunt Carrie checking her out? Did she approve of Edna? Since Carrie had raised Edward after the death of his parents when he was 10, her opinion mattered.

Flustered, Edna left the room with an unusual feeling. It was "weird and wonderful but scary and peculiar, too."

There they were, the student nurse and the returned soldier, both at a crossroads in their lives as they contemplated their futures. He had just recently left the horrors of war and was ready to begin the adult, settled part of life. She was ready to graduate, get a good job, and enjoy her independence.

Edna went off night duty, and in the meantime Edward was released from the hospital. He had found a job and moved to Lancaster, and the move signified THE END to the acquaintanceship, at least to the young nurse. It was just as well, she thought. After all, she didn't want to get serious about anyone for a while—years at least.

Edna might never have seen the charmer again if not for his cousin, Bitsy Barfield. Bitsy was Edna's supervisor, and one night she said, "Edward wants to know if you'll date him Saturday night."

After a short hesitation, she said, "Okay."

Their first date was at Ward's Steak House in Lugoff, and they dated regularly for five months. Then he stopped calling. Not the kind of woman who believed in chasing a man, Edna held her chin high, stood up straight, brushed off her shoulders, and moved on. Figuring it was over, she even dated once or twice, and one night as she and a date walked out of a building, there was Edward leaning up against a meter, watching her.

Still no contact.

Then Aunt Carrie was admitted to the hospital, and Edna dropped by her room to see her. What was the harm in that? After all, the issue wasn't with Aunt Carrie but with her personality-plus nephew.

And there he sat, comfortably ensconced in a chair in Carrie's room. Embarrassed, Edna left the room, and Edward soon followed her and asked her to see a movie. Just like that. And just like that, she said yes.

Still a little bruised and confused about the month's absence, Edna was wary at first. Why had he stopped calling when everything seemed to be fine? He admitted that he had been a bit hurt and muddled too. He loved her, and yet she would not/did not tell him that she loved him. He was ready to settle down and begin the next chapter of his life *with her*, and she didn't appear to be as serious as he. She hadn't even told him that she loved him.

Surprised by his admission, Edna confessed that she wasn't really ready to settle down. Her goal was to get a good job and enjoy her independence. While she didn't emphatically say NO to his marriage proposal, Edna told Edward that while she wasn't opposed to the idea, she wanted to work a little while first.

This time around, Edward was more patient. He asked her again. She was in love and wanted to spend her life with this man; she just wasn't ready to do it quite yet. A family member told her, "You know, I don't think Edward's going to ask you again." He did, though.

The next time Edward proposed, it was on the telephone. Something about that medium of communication instead of the face-to-face variety convinced Edna of the truism, "Three strikes and you're out."

She said yes.

The Crolleys got married on December 25, 1946 and began their life together in Lancaster after a short honeymoon at the Wade Hampton Inn in Columbia. They soon moved back to Camden where they both saw their hopes and dreams come to fruition. He settled down as a family man with three children and six grandchildren, and she, his helpmeet, worked as a nurse all of her professional life.

Many Camdenites have been influenced by Dr. Paul Wood and his nurse, Edna Crolley. A devoted wife and mother, she always retained her independent spirit. A lovely home now sits on the site of the old hospital, which was razed to the ground decades ago. Still, Mrs. Crolley often drives by and recalls the charming patient she met on the corner of Union and Fair.

The Fourth Ingredient
Kathryn Etters Lovatt

When I think of my mother, she rises up in my mind's eye like one of the photographs of her I keep in my bookcase. Sometimes she wears the pure silver hair of her eighties; more often, she's salt and pepper, one wild white streak from part to temple.

No matter her guise, she nearly always stands at the stove, her back bent over whatever she happens to be cooking. I often wonder if this isn't something of a universal vision, where all mommies and grandmas, mee-maws and nanas prepare to feed us, their very own tired and hungry, the food of our memories.

Here in the South, we collectively yearn for way-back-when, a time tinged with streak of lean and the dark flavors of cast iron skillets. We seek satisfaction in the buffet lines of home-style restaurants where they shamelessly fill the bar with vats of salad and vegetables from giant cans. On occasion, this desperate situation forces some of us into the hard labor of country cooking. There, one governing rule prevails: no shortcuts.

In the house where I grew up, top round was pounded thin under the fading edge of a Golden Wheat saucer, the lone survivor of my grandmother's laundry soap china. Cubed steak, tenderized and nicely packaged by a butcher, was rebuffed as substandard. Although I brought recipes featuring casseroles and no-bake pies from the home economics class my school required girls to take, no one-dish meals, noodle entrees or anything that involved the addition of a can of creamed soup ever came to the table. We ate roasts, beef or pork, vegetables picked in season or put in plastic boxes for the freezer.

By far, everyone's favorite was the chicken my mother brined, dredged and lightly fried. The lament of the last decades of her life was the loss of old-timey fryers. She kept an eye out for reasonable sized birds, ones with middling drumsticks and normal-size breasts. She went to every grocer in town until she found exactly what she wanted of any ingredient. One blazing hot summer, after shuttling her to Winn-Dixie, Bi-Lo, IGA, and Piggly Wiggly in search of a bag of passable onions, I turned in exasperation to my daughter. "This," I said, "is why I write."

My mother had her own calling. She read cookbooks like daily devotionals and kept in a drawer by her chair a few select ones: the chalky blue tome, *Joy of Cooking*, a raggedy *Good Housekeeping, Rumford Complete,* and Fanny Farmer's *Boston School of Cooking.* An oversized rubber band held together a collection of recipes from an ambitious junior league. She liked to peruse recipes, but she made most things by the tried and true.

I can picture her elbow-deep in cornbread dressing, rolling strips of dumpling, testing the soft-ball stage of fudge icing in a cup of cold water. She cooked everything from the ordinary to the exotic: speckled butterbeans and catfish, rabbit and dove, saddle of venison, ducks and geese and rhubarb, cream puffs and rarebits.

Camden Writers

But of all the foods she fried or baked or steamed, I miss her biscuits most. My mother's biscuits. Biscuits like no other. And I, who have spent the last six years trying to duplicate them, would know.

"Try one," she always said as she pulled them from the oven. "They might not be any good." But they always were. I thought her guilty of false modesty, but now I understand. With biscuits, you never *do* know if they'll turn out.

Oh, it sounds simple enough.

A biscuit, after all, contains three basic ingredients: self-rising flour, shortening, and milk. There is no mystery in what goes in the bowl. Why then have so many of my own biscuits gone into the bellies of my brother's goats? Because they rise too high. They cook too fine. Because they lack the tender sponge of my mother's bread. And when you've enjoyed the great good luck of breaking open those biscuits and smelling the aroma that blooms out, you are spoiled forever. Her biscuits came out crisp and thin and, although they needed nothing more than eating, they stood up to slathers of butter, ladles of gravy, a sop.

Theoretically, I know quite a lot about biscuits.

I have received no scarcity of advice on how to make the perfect pan. Friends, family, the backs of flour bags and the worldwide web all chime in. They suggest I use too much shortening. Or too little. Tell me to add butter or a big spoon of sugar. Try Adluh, White Lilly, Pillsbury Grands out of the freezer case. Heavy on direction, light on results.

74

I've sought the blessing of my mother's sifter, thought her ancient baking pan might be the charm. I've tried talking to her in heaven as well as speaking positive affirmations. "All right," I say as I get ready. "This is the day. This sticky mess in my hands will make the perfect batch." But I am wrong, wrong, and wrong again.

So I am left trying. Trying and almost always failing. Trying again. Getting closer. It is very much like writing in that way. And, come to think of it, very much like everything else.

I suppose I should have learned from her while she was alive to show me the way, but some deep superstition abided in me then. Biscuits were her bailiwick, and as long as no one else could make them half as well, she'd have to stick around and fix them herself. Until she was 88, she did exactly that. And then it was too late.

This much I know: my mother worked by instinct and experience and without benefit of measure, rolling pin or cutter. She worked light and fast,

> *My mother had her own calling. She read cookbooks like daily devotionals...*

throwing together a dough so moist, she floured her own hands before she patted them into shape. Only then did she set the oven to 500 degrees. Her perfect circles rested for those preheating minutes, and just before she shoved them into bake, she flattened each with the tips of her fingers.

There, in her final deliberate gesture, lies the true secret of my mother's biscuits. Her print made the difference, the sweet oil of her experienced hand. And for that ingredient, there is no substitute.

Skip-it
Brenda Bevan Remmes

A stoic woman in a starched high neck dress sits with a book in her hand surrounded by five attentive children. The woman, Alice Warren, had fled the fires in Atlanta to move in with her sister to a plantation home built three years prior to the firing on Fort Sumter. Shortly

thereafter, they could no longer make the mortgage payments. As rumors swirled that Sherman's men were burning their way through Columbia and headed for Camden, my great-great grandfather bundled the books in burlap bags, looped ropes at the top and hoisted them down from the attic into the six hollow columns. The women and children survived the war. Their men did not. Neither did the books.

The next picture that includes a book is on the lap of my great-grandparents, looking very Presbyterian. I'm told she read to the children exclusively from the Bible.

And then along came Molly. Molly's family had worked in the fields and kitchens through three generations, and after slaves were freed, they stayed to do the only work they knew how. My grandmother, widowed at a young age, worked hard to keep the farm and a small landscaping business afloat. She had a cook and a baby nurse to watch over her six children while she spent her days outside tending to plants and the yards of other people. There was no money for pictures.

Instructed to read to the children whenever she could, Molly preferred to tell a story, but if reading was required, so be it, she'd read. Her own education had been limited by her family's need to bring in enough money to feed them all. While the white children were in school, she cleaned houses. When they got home, she read them stories.

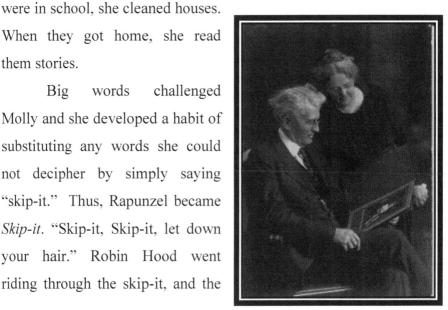

Big words challenged Molly and she developed a habit of substituting any words she could not decipher by simply saying "skip-it." Thus, Rapunzel became *Skip-it*. "Skip-it, Skip-it, let down your hair." Robin Hood went riding through the skip-it, and the fairy godmother in Cinderella would wave her magic wand and say "skip-it." She said she was teaching the children an important lesson in life: to understand what people meant, not what they said.

I now have a lovely four year old grandson who is being raised in London and enunciates his words with British precision. I still have my southern drawl. I say budder. He says BUTter. Sometimes we don't understand one another.

He loves books and he likes order and correctness, but he tweaks my English a bit too frequently for my liking. "BB," he calls me. "BB, you read that wrong."

"No, I didn't," I protest.

"It's not a DOE-waah." Red bangs scatter across big blue eyes. "It's a D...D...D" He says the D sound phonetically as his mother has taught him. "OR..OR...DOOR."

"No," I insist, teasing him. "They say it wrong over here."

He pounds his tiny fist on the book. "No, they don't."

"Tell you what," I say, "If I'm not saying a word right, just say *skip-it.*

"Skip-it?" He questions. "What's that?"

"It means you know what I mean, not what I say."

He mulls this over for a few seconds. "Okay," he agrees with a nod. "Skip it."

I'm there for several more days with skip-it incorporated between the two of us like a secret code.

When I get ready to leave, I kneel to the floor and hold out my arms. "How about a hug?"

"Skip it," he says flashing a devilish grin over his shoulder as he runs in the opposite direction.

"What did you say to your grandmother?" my son's voice booms through the hallway.

"No, no," I hurriedly jump to my grandson's defense. "He's not being rude, he's reading between the lines."

"Which means?" my son asks.

"He's learning a Southern tradition."

An Extraordinary Sunday
Jayne Padgett Bowers

As I pushed the back door open after church that Sunday, there stood one of my favorite people, Izzie Connell. A retired teacher and the matriarch of a large family, she was serenely standing right outside of the door, smiling and speaking to people as they exited the building. We chatted a few seconds, and then J.C. walked out. Her husband of nearly 60 years, he reached for her hand, smiled at me, and said, "It's my job to keep this lady happy." She softly laughed, and the two of them walked hand-in-hand towards their car.

I stood watching and wondering. How had they kept love alive all those decades? Had it truly been love at first sight for them? According to the story she often tells, yes. Izzie claims that she knew J.C. would be the father of her children on a Sunday afternoon in 1953, the first time that she met him. "In that case," she said, "I figured I better get to know him a little better."

It was an ordinary October Sunday, and Izzie was working in the dorm office. A Winthrop student, she was anxious to finish the term and go home for the holidays. She'd missed everyone and was especially concerned about her mother. If only she had transportation, some way to get to Camden to check on her mother, maybe her jangled nerves could unwind.

As she busied herself in the office, a surprise visitor appeared, her sister Ruby. She and her husband Cotton lived in Charlotte and had decided to go to Camden for the day. On impulse, they swung by the college on the slim chance that Izzie would be free to tag along. The fates were with the sisters that day because Izzie was soon able to find another student to switch schedules with her. Off the threesome headed to Camden, chatting gaily as they caught up with each other's lives.

Upon arrival at the Thompson home, the travelers were disappointed to find a deserted house. Not a soul was at home. A phone call soon revealed the family's whereabouts. Izzie and Ruby's parents were at the Connell's home, paying their respects to the family whose mother had died.

The Connell home wasn't too far away, and the trio once again climbed in the car and went for a ride, this time a short one. As they rode into the driveway, they spotted several parked cars and some people milling about in the yard. One person in particular grabbed Izzie's attention, a young man who had recently returned from military service.

She was immediately drawn to him and later declared that he was the best looking man she had ever seen. Izzie's father was one of the people standing in the yard, and he introduced the two young people. Izzie and J.C. shook hands politely. Was it her imagination, or did J.C. hold her hand a little longer than usual? This Sunday was turning into something not so ordinary after all.

Izzie recalls, "I heard a voice inside my head saying, 'This is the man you're going to marry.'"

I'm okay with that! she remembers thinking.

One of the Connell's daughters, Betty Joyce, came rushing out into the yard and hugged Ruby and Izzie. Upon observing this scene, the *best looking man* declared, "Well, I sure didn't get a reception like that."

"I can fix that," Izzie said, and she turned to hug him. While embracing, she *knew* without a doubt that this man was to be her husband and father of her children. Admittedly, her feelings were a bit disconcerting. This man's mother had just passed away, and yet Izzie's magnetic attraction towards J.C. was unmistakable, and she knew the feeling was mutual.

Distance was their biggest challenge. Izzie was in Rock Hill, and J.C. was in Camden. Neither had a car. Still, they managed to see each other as often as possible. No stranger to hitch hiking, J.C. used his thumb to catch rides to Rock Hill, and although Izzie was concerned about his safety, the young romantic assured her that he'd be safe. He'd been all over the states and had never had any problems with people. Looking back, Izzie attributes J.C.'s safety to his innate goodness.

Months passed, and after Isabelle Thompson graduated from Winthrop College, she moved to Tampa to be near J.C. who was employed in an engineering firm there. They soon married, and J.C. decided to rejoin the military, thus embarking on a life that would take them around the world and provide many rich experiences.

The Connell's first son, Bob, was born before they left Florida, and J.C. remembers walking into the hospital room seeing Izzie cradling their infant son in her arms. He reminisces about how radiant she looked, her long auburn hair spilling out on the pillow. "And Bob was such a cute little baby," he recalls. Is that when he made the decision to rejoin the military? While several factors influenced J.C.'s choice, the touching scene of mother and child definitely played a role in reminding him of the awesome responsibility involved in raising a child.

Although there were challenges throughout the years, the couple thoroughly enjoyed the military life and all the enriching experiences it provided. "We got to see so much of this great world," Izzie said. She fondly remembers traveling by train to watch her sons participate in sporting events in Germany. "It was a lot different then. It's not like we jumped in a car and rode across town. It took some work and time to see them play, but it was so worth it."

Six children, 34 grandchildren, and 23 great-grandchildren later, the Connells still hold hands and marvel at that first meeting. Was it a coincidence that Ruby felt that she needed to stop in Rock Hill to pick up her younger sister?? Would Izzie and J.C. have met if she had not come to Camden on the day of his mother's passing? It's ironic that J.C. met the love of his life on the day he lost his mother. Or is it?

To the devoted couple holding hands leaving church that day, the answer to all the above questions is no. They know invisible forces were at work behind the scenes to bring them together on that extraordinary October Sunday. Indeed, they view their first meeting as a beneficent nod from above.

Hoover Soup
Douglas Wyant

Born in 1921, my parents grew up during the Great Depression— Mother, on a farm near Cassatt, South Carolina, and Daddy, on a farm near Green Sulphur Springs, West Virginia.

Mother was the youngest of six children. When she was only four years old, she lost her mother, who died of cancer at forty. Although they might only have grits for breakfast and beans and cornbread for supper, Mother said there was always food on the table at mealtime.

Daddy remembered that they often ate bread and *with-it*, as in bread with gravy or bread with butter and jam. He had fourteen siblings—seven brothers and seven sisters. When unexpected guests showed up at supper time, his father said, "We'll sit up with you all night to keep you from going to bed hungry."

But his mother just added a little more water to the soup.

In memory of my parents, Wilma Bradley Wyant and Elbert "Shorty" Wyant.

Changing Traditions
Jayne Padgett Bowers

Throughout the 1950's and 60's, our family of six and my aunt's family of eight gathered at my paternal grandparents' home on Christmas Eve for a delightful evening of merry making. As the family grew, spouses and small children began making their appearance, and my grandparents' small house seemed to be bursting at the seams. I LOVED the yearly event and began looking forward to it around Halloween.

We listened to stories of Christmases past, caught up on each other's lives, and filled up on the delicious victuals my grandmother had prepared. My personal favorite was a pound cake chock full of walnuts. And candy. It was sweet coconut covered with the smoothest, tastiest chocolate I've ever sampled. How did my grandmother get the chocolate so slick and perfect? Even today with microwaves and easily melted chocolate, my candy creations can't compare to Beatrice's.

My grandparents didn't have much money, and the only material gifts I recall receiving from them were sweaters that my grandmother had lovingly crocheted throughout the year. In later years, we all received money. It was only a few dollars, but what those dollars represented was priceless: love. Days ahead of time, my grandparents went to the bank and got enough cash to put from three to five dollars in each grandchild and great grandchild's envelope, the kind with an oval opening in the front. New in-laws got the same gift.

While the gifts were appreciated, what we all treasured the most was simply being with family. Whether sitting around the large oak table or having "side" conversations with various family members, we sensed our connection and the bond that brought us back to this same location every year. Somehow it fortified us as we separated for our individual life paths after the holiday.

For a few years, our family lived next door to my grandparents, and at some point in the evening grown-ups began talking about where Santa was and when he'd likely arrive in Camden. Occasionally, one of them would make a point of gazing out of the window and calling attention to lights in the sky directly above our house. "Are those the lights of Santa's sleigh?" one of the grown ups would wonder aloud. A naïve and trusting child, I fell for the trick and was usually the first to say, "Let's go home so he can come."

Christmas Day brought us back to my grandparents' house. This time there was a real meal, a feast fit for kings with contributions from my mother and aunt. So many people attended that all of us could not sit around the dining room table, and consequently many of the children got relegated to the floor in an adjoining room. Did that bother us? Not one iota. We were delighted to be engaged this unusual dining situation, an indoor picnic for kids only. What are a few green beans, a little sloshed gravy, and biscuit crumbs on the floor in the grand scheme of things? What gaiety! What Christmas cheer! A jolly good time was had by all...or so I imagined.

Then one year everything changed. Home from Winthrop for the holidays, I noticed that my mother wasn't in the kitchen whipping up a cake or baking those tasty lady fingers that only she could create to perfection, slightly browned with a single pecan half in the middle of each. The consummate homemaker, my mother was performing daily maintenance tasks like cooking for a family of six, but there was nothing extra going on. No mac and cheese for MaMa and Granddaddy Padgett's annual gala events. What was up with that?

On the 23rd, we learned that my mother had no plans to accompany the family to her in-laws' home for the festivities. No amount of pleading would change her mind. Oblivious to goings-on and their significance, I had not ever noticed that we had *never* spent a single holiday with her family. Not one. And beyond the predawn discovery of Santa's yearly generosity, we had never spent Christmas day in our own home.

In 1970, Christmas celebrations as we had always known them were history. Was my mother having a midlife crisis? Or perhaps she had realized the truth of the platitude: "If it is to be it's up to me." Whatever the source of her refusal to budge, my sweet mama's decision didn't go over well with her mother-in-law. She took Mama's nonattendance personally while the rest of us were just confused by this seemingly sudden change of heart.

Little did any of us realize the far-reaching ramifications of my mother's Christmas decision. The next year all six of us made the annual Christmas Eve visit and enjoyed the sugary desserts and warm camaraderie, but the next day marked a break in tradition. My grandparents joined us at our home for Christmas dinner, my grandmother sullen and sulky and my mother happy but anxious. Although I was probably 22 by this time, I still didn't have the depth to understand the emotional undercurrents of the day. I just knew that something had shifted.

At first I missed the frenzied good cheer shared with my extended family, but that was soon overshadowed by the pride I felt in my mother for taking a stance and establishing her position as matriarch of her growing family.

More than Fruitcake

I knew before I got out of bed," she says, turning away from the window with a purposeful excitement in her eyes. "The courthouse bell sounded so cold and clear. And there were no birds singing; they've gone to warmer country, yes indeed. Oh, Buddy, stop stuffing biscuit and fetch our buggy. We've thirty cakes to bake."

It's always the same: a morning arrives in November, and my friend, as though officially inaugurating the Christmas time of year that exhilarates her imagination and fuels the blaze of her heart, announces: "It's fruitcake weather! Fetch our buggy. Help me find my hat."

Truman Capote
A Christmas Memory

Camden Writers

More than Fruitcake
Kathryn Etters Lovatt

My history with fruitcake is as long and layered as my memory, and it begins with my grandfather.

Keistler Campbell Etters managed to acquire a bit of money and a little land in his time. He built a solid house in the Sand Hills and dressed in suits from Sheorn's. He wore calfskin wingtips, special-ordered for his narrow feet. He kept his winter hats in their fancy boxes until, brushing down their creases and satin trims, he fit them on his head. One summer hat that I remember sported a single feather in the band, so slight and delicate a scant breeze would ruffle life back into its edges.

He grew accustomed to many fine things, but when it came to eating, the simple foods of his younger, hardscrabble life remained his favorites. For breakfast, he liked a slice of mush or a plate of brains and eggs. Midday, he preferred dried peas or beans accompanied by a cake of cornbread big enough for leftovers. For supper, he routinely crumbled a stale wedge in a bowl of cold milk.

Although loyal to his regular fare, he developed a taste for more exotic foods like deviled crab and oysters—in stew or fried—fresh coconuts, steamed asparagus with hollandaise, and how he loved a fruitcake.

In a pinch, he dunked pieces of early arrival Claxtons—the only brand readily available in grocery aisles—into the deep saucer of his coffee cup. And once, far in advance of the holidays, my Uncle Floyd sent him a shiny round cake from California. A surprising sunburst of almonds and whole dates decorated the top. Never ones to snub even commercial varieties and perhaps overly optimistic they might hit upon something equal to homemade, my family dug in. Over the years, such a quest led them to order from abbeys and brethren, from boutique bakeries and one time, out of Texas. I even brought holiday cakes home from London, although the streak of marzipan icing on the popular Marks and Spencers' brand took getting used to or, if that proved impossible, peeling off.

But in our heart of hearts, we always understood that if we wanted the real thing, we needed to look to the old recipes. And of those, we had plenty. We found them (and continue to discover them) in binders and on note cards, scribbled on the back of envelopes, typed out on paper so absurdly thin it earned the name "onion-skin."

From my mother's mother, Waco, I have two originals. In the days when lead lasted as long as ink, she wrote down in pencil a list of ingredients. Here and there are the most rudimentary of guidelines, and in her plain hand, simple and direct as she was, she added what she forgot to say earlier as she went along. The task of making order and sense was left up to the baker.

Grandmother prepared both dark and white, neither of which I cared for until I learned to spot the bits of bitter citron and roll them aside. She made a huge batch of the more familiar dark, filling a basin-like bowl with candied fruits, raisins, currants, watermelon rind, and homemade fig preserves. Over this, she drenched an overnight marinade of grape juice spiked with rosewater. A cloth remnant from Kendall Mills kept fruit flies at bay until the next day. She added flour browned in the skillet, pecans, English walnuts, Brazil nuts, grated chocolate, a litany of spices, dozens of eggs, and pounds of butter. These steamed cakes took days of attention. After my grandmother died, my mother and I modified the recipe, omitting the hard-to-come-by rosewater and homemade preserves: not a disaster, by any means, but not a triumph.

Still, every few years, my husband Dan pulls the big speckled bowl off the top of the cabinets as we gather our energy and go to work on one handed-down recipe or another. Results are generally reasonable, which seems totally unreasonable considering the time and energy, not to mention money, spent. But without fail, the process of preparation stirs up a host of memories.

I can see my Uncle Harrington, his silver hair parted down the middle, wire-rimmed glasses that made him look like a grand old poet. He baked his fruitcakes in loaf pans and fed them jiggers of spirits on a regular basis. On a fall afternoon—always a Sunday—he would trot a cake and a bottle of his homemade wine to my grandparents' house. What I remember best is how grandly he presented his offering. He would set the cake on the table as if it were the great Dickensian goose, and his lips would twitch as he unwound layers of cheesecloth. The smell stirred by the unfolding of that musky cocoon was as dark and mysterious as the thimble of red nectar he poured in everyone's glass, including mine.

My mother-in-law used to mail us a fruitcake from her home in Montana every year. When the box arrived, Dan's hand would glide right by the parcels of divinity and fudge to lift out five pounds of double-wrapped deliciousness. What we couldn't eat, we froze. Years ago, on a spring vacation at The Homestead in Virginia, we discovered that good fruitcake is good any old time. The restaurant in that celebrated resort served theirs year 'round with a glass of port and a wedge of English Cheddar.

Not everyone shares my enthusiasm for fruitcake. While some mouths water at the prospect, others turn inside out. More than a few people I know think it best served as a punch line. Year after year, didn't Johnny Carson joke that only one fruitcake actually existed? People just rewrapped it, he said, and passed it back around.

To that I say, *pass it over here.*

In our house, fruitcake is not so much a food as it is a symbol. Like Truman Capote's cousin, Sook, we begin in early fall to look for a shift in weather, a sign the season is officially upon us. We read again all the versions of our old recipes and find the ones with marginal warnings and corrections from previous attempts, but, without fail, we always make at least one batch of Cynthia DeFusco's fruitcake.

Thirty-plus years ago, this friend shared her recipe with me, so, naturally, we called it "Cynthia's Fruitcake." But one memorable December evening, our rescue dog, Holly, nosed her way into the dining room. She steadied herself on the table, and with her long reach, pulled both cakes within striking distance. She spared no crumb, leaving only a dribble of bright foil beneath a chair leg. Since that event, the cake, which is gloriously uncomplicated, carries her name. I don't believe Cynthia, a great lover of big dogs, would mind.

As we enter this holiday season, I expect we'll laugh again about our sweet dog's ravenous appetite, although we regret how ghastly sick that last holiday binge made her. My father might recall the years we gathered pecans off Hasty Road, from my great aunt's trees, and the effort it took to crack so many. He will know of other times, before me, when sugar was hard to come by and young men were either coming from or going to war. I will think back to the day I discovered rosewater in an international food store, and how my mother, uncapping the bottle and putting the top under her nose, smiled at her own memories.

Although Holly is gone now, and my uncle and my grandmother, my mother and Dan's, this holiday, like all the others, we will bring out the sharp cheese and good port and, if we have been able to muster enough energy for marathon baking, different kinds of fruitcake. We will gather around the table where, year after year, this small ritual brings us all, those here and those lost, back together.

Holly's Fruitcake

1 pound chopped pitted dates

1 pound chopped pecans

½ pound each candied cherries and candied pineapple, chopped

1 cup sugar

1 cup all purpose flour

2 teaspoons baking powder

1 teaspoon ground nutmeg

½ teaspoon salt

4 eggs, beaten

1 teaspoon vanilla

Combine dates, pecans, cherries and pineapple in large bowl.

Mix dry ingredients and add to fruit and nut mixture, stirring well.

Blend in beaten eggs and vanilla.

Spoon batter into greased and brown-paper lined 10-inch tube pan.

Bake at 275 degrees for 2 hours or until golden brown and firm.

For loaf pans, bake at same temperature, adjusting time.

People who love to eat are always the best people
Julia Child

COWBOY CAKE
Paddy Bell

There is not enough clove, cinnamon, or nutmeg on the planet to disguise the unnamed innards of that concoction known as mincemeat pie. Civilized recipes might list a bit of beef suet as an ingredient, but Grandma Mahoney's version was closer to ground up hog's head. In the early 1950s, as a five-year old child, the mere mention of this traditional holiday dessert of hers gave me the creeps. And all these years later, the thought of it still produces a shiver. Evidently not so much for the fifteen or so adult Mahoney's who voraciously devoured the mincemeat as well as the pumpkin and apple pies baked by Grandma. Later I began to realize that those fillings were just an excuse to get to the main attraction – the flaky lard-laden crust.

Lard was Grandma's mainstay. It lived in a red-checkered can on the pantry floor on the left under the knotty pine quarter shelves sagging from the weight of her canned jellies, sauces, fruits, and vegetables. The lard can was sturdy enough to sit on and tall enough to stand on to reach an upper shelf where another tin container held a stash of hard candies, the kind meant to be leisurely enjoyed on the tongue until they totally liquefied. I was never that disciplined. Crack. Crunch. The crystal pellets of cherry, raspberry, and licorice were hastily gobbled down. For me, the peppermint ones reminded me of toothpaste, so I snubbed them. No thanks.

On the other hand, I'd pick the candy stash clean of those heavenly lemon drops with the powdery-sugar coating, never bothering to chew, but just sucking off that delicious outer layer and swallowing the nuggets whole. A second, third, and sometimes fourth would be popped as I balanced on the lard can, keeping ears wide open for potential brother or cousin interlopers. At the end of my feast I carefully coaxed the lard can back into its exact position, respectful that the treasure inside the tin had something to do with enticing the likes of adults to eat mincemeat, pretending to like it just for the sake of the crust. Dad, of course, really did like it in view of his near starvation in a World War II prison camp. After scavenging for grubs, cockroaches, and putrid cabbage stalks, he had no problem with mincemeat.

While grandparents, parents, aunts, uncles, and assorted other adults enjoyed pie in the dining room, seven or eight grandchildren sat at the children's table in the kitchen, anticipating the presentation of Grandma's glorious creation for kids only, one strictly off-limits to our elders - Cowboy Cake!

Grandma ceremoniously placed the still-warm cake pan in the center of the grey-speckled Formica table with chrome legs. That table, with the easy wipe-clean top, was a gesture from Grandpa to eliminate the need for Grandma's starching and ironing of tablecloths she liked to use every day. She gave in a little, but on holidays, Sundays, and momentous events, the Formica top was draped with a crisp, clean linen. On these same days, she insisted that her fine white china with clusters of blue flowers circling the edges was used by all.

Since the china plate count fell far below the people head count, the solution was to eat in turns and wash plates in shifts. I recall the grumblings of an aunt as she sudsyed clean the plates at the big farm sink. "This here's plain stupidity, Maw. We ought to use those daily dishes just sitting there in the corner cupboard!" With no compromise on the matter for Grandma, that's where the daily dishes remained as she admonished, "Special occasions, special china, no matter how long it takes for all to eat. Now you just keep on, and thank the good Lord you got an indoor sink and hot water to be washing those plates in!" The two stippled and chipped plates that I have on my china hutch are among my priceless treasures, especially remembering the Cowboy Cake that they once held.

As Grandma cut and served us square pieces on her pretty china, our first thoughts were always to pick up the cake and wolf it down, but the flaky goodness that only lard can provide forced the use of a fork. I soon learned the trick of pressing the back of the tines into the crumbs left on the plate to savor every last tidbit. Parents had no say-so in requests for seconds. Only Grandma could approve, which she always did. I confess to eyeballing that cake pan as the contents dwindled to calculate what might be left for supper. Like the loaves and fishes, there was always plenty to satisfy and then some, thanks to our vigilance in fending off the family's rogue uncle – the trickster who loved to woozle and tease us nieces and nephews.

It was tradition that at every gathering he would skulk into the kitchen, see our crumb-covered faces, let out a war cry and yell, "Yum! Cowboy Cake! For me!" He clutched a big fork in his fist and lunged at the table while we all screamed, "No! Go away! Help, Grandma, help!"

Hunched over, whooping and hollering like a savage, he made wild tomahawk jabs at the Cowboy Cake as we'd circle the wagons and close ranks to protect the sacred cake. Screams soon turned to giggles, as we knew he didn't have a chance for even the tiniest nibble of Cowboy Cake. He'd pretend utter heartbreak and leave the kitchen shedding crocodile tears, boo-hooing, his loss—again.

Sadly, the secret to the naming of Cowboy Cake lies with Grandma, who has been gone for some thirty years. There is no one from her time left to ask. Best guess is that the name is due to the simplicity of style and ingredients that allows for any pioneer, homesteader, or chuck wagon cook to rassle it up. Its closest relative would be a typical coffee cake with a cinnamon-sugar crumble on top – no frosting, frills, or fluff.

This Thanksgiving or Christmas I believe I'll make a Cowboy Cake in case any children pop in. But the joy, the raucous trappings of too much family and too little china, the rowdy uncle, the old Formica table, and especially the red-checkered lard can that added to the wonder of cowboy cake will be missing. The kids-only rule will be missing as well, as I fully intend to test the back-of-the-fork tine maneuver to gather every tasty lard-laden crumb.

Cowboy Cake

2 ½ cups flour
2 cups brown sugar
½ teaspoon salt
2/3 cups shortening (Crisco or the real deal - lard!)

Mix the above and save ½ cup for topping.   To the rest add the following, mix, and pour into a greased 9 x 13 pan. Crumble the topping over and bake in a 350-degree oven for 30-45 minutes.

2 teaspoon. baking powder
½ teaspoon nutmeg
½ teaspoon. cinnamon
½ teaspoon soda
2 eggs
1 cup sour milk (add 1 tablespoon lemon juice or vinegar to 1 cup regular milk)

What's for Dessert?
Paddy Bell

"So what's for dessert tonight, Sweetie?" Dad asked my Mom that evening as he did every day.

"Spiced tapioca, thumb-print cookies, Yankee notions, and rhubarb pie."

"Oh, not much time for baking today, huh?"

That's right–these would be considered meager offerings in my mother's kitchen and by my family's standards. Tapioca was considered something out of the dairy food-group, so was handily dismissed. Thumb-print cookies, or ANY cookie for that matter, fell into a dessert sub-group, little more than a snack. And Yankee notions, baked pie dough remnants slathered in butter, cinnamon and sugar, were regarded as left-over scraps and did not qualify as a true dessert, yummy though they were. So on that night, the only chance for a bona fide offering of a delicacy was rhubarb pie.

It was by chance, indeed, thanks to my four-year old brother, Danny, who did some early morning weeding at a neighbor's garden. An elderly couple who lived three doors down had a carefully tended backyard garden, featuring several rows of tall crimson stalks of rhubarb thriving in rich black Ohio soil. When Danny busted in our backdoor, arms loaded with leafy fronds, crispy stalks, and hairy roots, his clothes and shoes smudged with dirt, he proudly announced, "Mommy, look! I weeded Mrs. Hyers garden for her!"

The "weeds" were none other than her prize rhubarb. Mom got to work, wrote a note pleading forgiveness for her son, and carried her picnic basket holding four freshly baked pies to the Hyers. Danny offered his apologies, and Mrs. Hyer sweetly said, "Oh, my dear boy, you are welcome to weed our garden any time if these pies are the result!" She kept three and insisted that Mom carry one pie back for us to enjoy.

Although much appreciated as a fruity dessert in this instance, rhubarb, like tomatoes, can suffer a fruit/vegetable identity crisis. It can be pickled, stewed, served in a salad for its celery-like crunch, or as a relish. Had Dad been of that persuasion, despite the sugary custard filling in the flaky crust, he might have decreed rhubarb as a mere side for a pork roast. Then we would have been left with no dessert at all. Horrors!

Sweets simply played a prominent role in our lives. Mom was a fantastic cook and even better baker, so cakes, pies, cream puffs, tarts and more were ever present, yet never taken for granted. Desserts were earned after eating a well-rounded meal of meat, vegetables, and salad, but were not just relegated to a finale for evening meals, and could appear when least expected. My mother-in-law commented on a visit to my parent's home shortly after Rick and I married, "I think I'm going to like these people. They eat pecan pie for breakfast."

The particular night in question, with the rhubarb pie standing as the lone potential dessert offering, the situation improved dramatically as we sat down for dinner and beheld a platter of fried chicken, a Pyrex bowl of ham-hocked green beans, and a huge crock of hot mashed potatoes, crowned with a generous pat of butter that was well on its way to a full melt. Oh yes, we knew…hoped…what awaited. Dad, my two brothers, and I wilily cut our eyes at each other and smiled like a litter of Cheshire cats as we prayed the blessing.

We always ate family style, passing heavy bowls of food, and this evening, we carefully watched each other and took measure of the helpings of mashed potatoes plopping onto plates. Second servings were even more closely calculated. There seemed to be more silence than usual as well, the air heavy with expectation. Dad's untucking of his napkin from his collar and final wipe of his mouth was the signal we eagerly anticipated. Mom would then ever so slowly peer into the mashed potato serving dish to study the remains. Despite our fears that maybe, just maybe, too many enjoyed too much, she'd always proclaim, "Looks like there'll be donuts tonight."

"Hooray!" we all screamed with relief.

There would be no shortage of help in clearing the table, washing and drying dishes, and making ready the sparse amount of counter space for Mom to get busy. Unbeknownst to us she had earlier completed the prep for the donuts and two mixing bowls were chilling in the refrigerator, awaiting the secret ingredient – mashed potatoes!

Dad retired to the living room to read the paper, and my brothers and I were shooed out of the kitchen to busy ourselves with a game or coloring books. What seemed an eternity was truly only minutes, until Mom called us back to the kitchen for donut duty. The hammered cast-iron roaster, which doubled as a deep fryer, was faintly droning on the range top as Mom readied the dough. We took turns with the red-handled donut cutter, careful to release the holes and not waste one little bit. But we were not allowed anywhere near the now-bubbling roaster as Mom dropped the holes and the donuts into the oil.

There is nothing in the world as pleasant as the sizzle and scrumptious aroma of frying dough. Those donuts would rise to the surface, almost like they were trying to escape, and Mom would vigilantly turn them until they reached the ideal shade of gold. She instinctively knew when they'd had enough, and she lifted them out at the perfect stage of crispy outer and light flaky inner. They were never soggy or heavy.

Once all the frying was done, and donuts were cooling on the wire baking racks, my brothers and I would gingerly drop holes and donuts into brown paper bags containing powdered sugar or a mixture of cinnamon and sugar. We'd give them a gentle shake, then set them back on the racks to cool completely. Somehow we worked elbow to elbow without teasing, fighting, arguing, or poking. Donuts brought out our very best behavior.

"Mmmmm. Smells like a bakery in here," Dad said as he joined us in the kitchen.

Glasses of icy cold milk, a considerable slew of napkins, and Mom's milk glass pedestal cake stand stacked high with sugary donuts and holes were set on the table. Dad also put away a healthy slice of rhubarb pie with a donut or two on the side. As for me, I wondered why in the world anyone would bother with dessert when they could be delighting in mashed potatoes like these.

Mrs. King's Fruitcake
Brenda Bevan Remmes

The identity of Mrs. King remains a mystery, but my family has had this recipe for years and I've never found it in print anywhere else. For anyone who swears they don't like fruitcake, this recipe will convert you into a believer of the Christmas tradition. Made with almost no flour, it is a concoction of nuts and fruit, held together by sweetened condensed milk. The work is in the chopping. Forget the wooden spoon for the mixing. Wash your hands and plunge into making this memorable treat.

1 pound chopped walnuts
1 pound chopped brazil nuts
1 pound chopped pecans
2 pounds. chopped seedless dates
2 pounds candied fruit
1 cup coconut
1 cup flour
2 cups Eagle Brand Condensed sweetened milk (1 can = 1.25 cups. Careful, don't use too much condensed milk.)

Put all the fruit in large bowl and dredge with flour.

Add all the other ingredients and combine thoroughly (I use my hands to make sure that the condensed milk is equally distributed throughout).

Spray six small loaf pans with Baker's Joy non-stick Spray.

Pack (really pack) each pan with ingredients so that there are no air pockets.

Bake at 325 for 1 hour and 15 minutes. Watch bottoms of fruitcakes. Don't let them burn. I generally cook mine for 1 hour and then turn off the oven and just let them sit for 15 minutes.

Wrap in tin foil and freeze. I freeze mine because they seem to hold firmer if I do that. Then I pull one at a time out, thaw and cut. Use either an electric knife or very sharp knife to cut. It's like cutting hard bread. The cake will crumble into small pieces if you're not careful, but who cares? It's delicious anyway you cut it.

Enjoy.

Hats and Cornbread

Jayne Padgett Bowers

On the first Thanksgiving without my mother, my siblings and other assorted family members gathered at our parents' house for a "take-in" meal. Although my father had predeceased her by two years, we all still thought of it as Mama and Daddy's house and weren't quite sure how to move on. On that Thursday, everyone brought a little something to add to the annual feast, and admittedly, it was a bit of a hodgepodge.

Before eating, we rummaged through some of our parents' belongings and found a hat for everyone to wear throughout the evening. It was fun to see what people chose. My brother Mike selected one of Daddy's National Guard hats, and my sister Ann opted for a vintage hat that made quite a fashion statement, a brown velvet chapeau with a huge decorative bow that sat right over the left ear. Sarah Beth, one of my nieces, donned a dusky pink pillbox to complement her pink sweater. She and Katherine, my other niece, carried some of Granny's purses around with them that day, remembering how their grandmother always made sure that her pocketbooks matched her shoes.

We wore our hats hoping to keep that holiday spirit alive. Did it work? Not really. The picture snapped by my son-in-law late that afternoon looks like everyone is having a good old time, but looks can be deceiving. Despite our fake smiles, we were all still heartbroken, our psyches raw with fresh grief.

It probably hit me for the first time that evening: My family holidays with kith and kin in the manner I had known all of my life were over. Sure, I'd share turkey and dressing, red velvet cake, and other seasonal fare with various relatives each year, but my mother's passing on October 20, 2000, marked the end of gatherings in the family home. *Marjorie Ann was the heart of it all. It was never the same after her passing.*

For a few years the eight of us, siblings and spouses, met in restaurants for a communal meal and gift exchange during the Christmas holidays. It was always more sad than jolly. The days of hearing, "Mama said to be there no later than 12:30," were over. So were conversations between her grandchildren and her about what they were to do PRONTO!

SHOWTIME!

"You kids go outside and play," she'd say.

"But we want to stay in here with you. Can I have a brownie?"

"No, you may not! I want you children to plan a program for everyone to enjoy. Now skedaddle and get to work on it."

"But what kind of program, Granny?"

"That's up to you. Just scoot. NOW!"

And wow, there were quite a few ingenious productions! From designing unique costumes to writing original scripts, Granny's grandkids were quite creative and entertaining. I can still hear little Ben singing, "Skinny Marinky Dinky Dink" and remember how cute he looked as he did the arm movements for the sun and moon. I can also see the four oldest grandchildren dressed as Indians and Pilgrims as they recited a novel Thanksgiving poem.

And I doubt seriously that anyone will ever forget 3-year-old John David standing on a stool "preaching" to the living room congregation with confidence and fervor. A Gideon Bible clutched in one tiny hand, the preschooler held us rapt as we watched his performance. Was this perhaps a foreshadowing of his later pursuit of an apologetics degree in seminary?

For the last few Christmases of her life, my mother began to reflect on the excess of the season and decided that it was all too much. The food, the over-the-top gifts, the tinsel—all of it. It disturbed her to think of hungry, homeless, cold people who were suffering while we had so much.

As a consequence, Mama decided to simplify our holiday menus. We had waffles and bacon for Christmas dinner one year and soup and sandwiches the next. The waffles were yummy, and we made accommodations for everyone's preferences. If you wanted blueberry, then blueberry it was. If you wanted whole wheat smeared with honey and peanut butter, you got it. It was a bit hectic in Granny's kitchen that year, and thankfully my niece Katherine was the unofficial chef and overseer of three waffle irons.

And the soup and sandwich year? As I recall, my sister and sisters-in-law concocted a variety of savory soups and provided fixings for several specialty sandwiches. So much for "keeping it simple." Interestingly, the children wanted chicken noodle soup from a can and PBJs. Even so, the younger set was a little picky about types of jelly, and Mama arranged to have Welch's grape for Paul and his young cousins.

My mother was an excellent cook. As a child, every single Christmas I'd sneak into the kitchen, quietly remove the top of the fudge tin, nab a piece of creamy fudge (with pecans), move the other pieces around so that she'd never notice the missing piece, replace the lid, and run out the back door before anyone knew what I was up to. Out of eyesight, I'd pop that heavenly concoction in my mouth and savor its delicious sweetness before nonchalantly waltzing back in.

These days I never fix fudge. Never. But every single holiday, I make my mother's cornbread stuffing. It's a way of keeping her with us. And naturally, I use her square cast iron skillet to bake the cornbread used in the dressing. I've sampled my share of dressings in my life, and hers was the best. Savory but not heavily seasoned with sage or poultry seasoning, it was perfect.

I was helping her put things away after a meal one evening, and as I covered the leftover dressing with foil, I asked, "How do you make this anyway?"

"It's not hard. Just mix some eggs, broth, celery, and chicken with your cornbread."

"My cornbread? You mean Jiffy?"

"Don't be silly, Jaynie. If you want to make my dressing, then you'll have to make my cornbread."

"Uh, okay. Could you tell me again exactly what to add and how much?"

Without further ado, she gave me the cornbread recipe, the same one that's found in *Home Cookin'*, a collection of recipes submitted by women of First Baptist Church of Camden in 1992. All profits from the sale of the cookbook were given to the World Hunger offering, and I'm happy that my beautiful mother was a part of that mission.

Granny's Corn Bread

Ingredients

1 cup all purpose flour
¾ cup cornmeal
2 ½ teaspoon baking powder'
¾ teaspoon salt
½ teaspoon soda
2 eggs
1 cup buttermilk
½ cup melted margarine

Instructions
Add eggs and buttermilk to dry ingredients
Melt margarine in iron skillet.
Add melted margarine to other ingredients and bake in iron skillet at 400 degrees until bread is nicely browned and left sides of skillet.

Serves 6 to 8.

As for the delectable stuffing, here are her exact words, the ones I scribbled in the front of a *Southern Living Annual Cookbook.* I've added my comments in Italics.

Cook chicken. She was a bit indefinite about how much and what kind (dark or white), but she used about three or four breasts.

Cool chicken and break apart (or cut into pieces).

Use the broth from chicken. If not enough, then add some from a can.

"How much?" I asked.

"Until it's the right consistency."

"Oh," I replied, too embarrassed to ask anything else.

Add:
Some celery.

Some? Not a huge celery fan, I chopped just enough to add some color.

Salt and pepper to taste.
Finely chopped onion.
Sage if you want it—just a smidge.

Add to crumbled cornbread and cook in 9 x 12 baking dish at 350 degrees for about an hour and 15 minutes or until it's brown on the top.

P. S. My mother taught me how to make cornbread and her yummy dressing. She also taught me the importance of family and tradition. She just didn't teach me how to put the holidays back together after loss. If she had tried, would I have listened? Would I have been an apt student? Probably not. At that time I was one of those shortsighted people who didn't realize that everything changes. Everything.

The Spatula Cake:
A New Southern Tradition
Martha Dabbs Greenway

Most folks know about a King cake. You know, that seasonal cake with the plastic baby Jesus baked in it. It's usually served in the days leading up to Lent and is especially popular for Mardi Gras. Nancy Lee, the next birthday gal in our group, grew up in Louisiana and often talked about baking a King cake.

There were seven of us who, after a soul-baring overnight trip to Savannah to stay in the 1895 Inn, decided to get together more often. Celebrating our birthdays seemed appropriate. We'd buy the honoree's lunch, bring a card—the more outrageous the better—no gifts, but the rest of the "rules" were vague. For the first two birthdays beautiful cakes were part of the celebration. Having only brought cards, enjoyed the food and the camaraderie, I asked Virginia—who not only brought the cake but also picked up the honoree's lunch tab— if I could help with the expenses.

"Why don't you bring the cake next time," she said with a smile.

"Sure," I replied, already regretting my response as I hadn't baked in years and didn't want to spend $40 at the bakery.

"Chocolate cake with buttercream frosting," was Nancy Lee's response to my what's your favorite query.

Soon I was rifling through old recipes and found one for chocolate sour cream pound cake. It was credited to Nena, my neighbor in Charlotte, which means I'd had the recipe for over forty years. It's possible it had been that long since I'd baked one. I gathered the ingredients and set aside the afternoon before the celebration for cake day. While the eggs and butter were warming to room temperature, I began to grease and flour the cake pan and since I was using a Bundt pan with those scalloped sides, I used a cooking spray instead of Crisco. I sprinkled it with flour and even though I turned the pan and slapped the sides to distribute the flour just like I'd seen my mama do, it seemed like clumps of flour were holding onto the creases of those scallops. I took the pan out to the back steps, and after a few beatings on the iron railing, it looked perfect.

Creaming the butter and sugar was the next step and sounded so easy, but soon small bits of sugared butter were flying out of the mixing bowl and onto the kitchen walls and countertop. Why didn't I watch that how-to YouTube video before rather than after making such a mess? Finally, it seemed sufficiently creamed, and I added the rest of the ingredients.

I poured the batter into the perfectly greased and floured pan. With the same spatula I had used to scrape down the sides of the bowl thus far, I was trying to get to the last of the batter when I saw that the tip of the spatula was gone. It must have gotten caught in the blades of the hand mixer. There was no going back. I didn't have enough ingredients to start over. Pouring it through a strainer would waste a lot of batter, and I'd be back banging the over-floured pan on the step railing again. *No,* I thought, *just bake it.*

The cake smelled good and looked good. The icing was easier to make than the cake and I found some colorful and crazy candles that worked. My friends laughed when I told the story and presented Nancy Lee with her "Spatula Cake," but I sensed a touch of apprehension as she sliced the cake and passed it around. Finally, the fifth slice ended up in front of me. Something looked a little strange and with the tip of my fork I was able to dislodge the missing piece of the spatula. We were all relieved but I'm not sure it's the start of a new Southern tradition.

Nena's Chocolate Sour Cream Pound Cake

1 cup butter

2 cups sugar

2 eggs

2 squares unsweetened baking chocolate, melted

2 teaspoons vanilla

2 teaspoons soda

2 1/2 cups plain flour, sifted

1/4 teaspoon salt

1 (8-ounce) carton sour cream

1 cup boiling water

Have all ingredients at room temperature. Cream butter and sugar, add eggs, melted chocolate and vanilla to creamed mixture.

Mix soda, flour and salt. Add to chocolate mixture alternately with sour cream.

Lastly, add 1 cup boiling water to everything and mix well.

Pour into a greased and floured tube pan and bake for 45 minutes, or until cake tests done, in a 325-degree oven. I find I have to bake mine at least 55 minutes. Cool cake completely and frost if desired.

Ski Slope Cake
Ari Dickinson

I have never enjoyed cooking, and find baking disastrous. Imagine how intimidated I felt when I married and moved to South Carolina to find that my mother-in-law, Fanny, was one of the great cooks of all time.

Every Sunday she served a dinner for family and friends which surpassed anything I was accustomed to even on holidays. The day's five vegetables in every color, served in one meal. That didn't count the pickles, relishes, salads, and aspics. Delectable meats and side dishes, urged on us lucky ones in second and third helpings. And the desserts! Coconut or chocolate or caramel cakes, exquisite layers perfectly stacked, pies and cobblers oozing with sweet fillings.

> And the desserts! Coconut or chocolate or caramel cakes, exquisite layers perfectly stacked, pies and cobblers oozing with sweet fillings.

Fortunately for my poor husband, Fanny fed us every Sunday for years, and he never said anything about our much less adequate diet in between.

I couldn't—wouldn't have dared to try to cook like that. And I never did, until after Fanny was gone, and my daughter insisted that we really must undertake my husband's favorite cake—Fanny's Chocolate Cream Cheese Layer Cake—for his birthday.

I resisted, but she was right, of course. I got on my hands and knees and excavated for my spring-form cake pans, wedding presents still in mint condition, unsullied and untried.

We found the recipe and did our best. The chocolate and cream cheese filling/frosting, we confirmed, was delicious. The cake layers contained chocolate and cream cheese, too, but somehow they were not as pleasing. They came out crooked and uneven. I like to think my oven was at least partly to blame. I get confused about where the line is crossed between vintage and antique, but it was almost fifty years old at the time, and hotter on the left side near the back. This, as you might guess, had never been an obstacle to me before!

We put the layers together as well as we could, but the result was definitely slanted. And the frosting, so delicious licked off our fingers, was slippery, so that the layers swooped and glided on each other, squeezing the frosting out between the seams.

Alas, our time was up. My husband and his birthday were upon us. Thinking quickly, we looked in our stash of plastic birthday decorations from store-bought cakes gone by, and passing over Minnie Mouse and the tutued dancing rabbit, seized on several miniature pine trees from an earlier camping theme. We set them on our "hill" and used a spatula to make a winding trail down the slant of the cake, a ski slope to warm any sportsman's heart.

As it turned out, the wobbly, crooked cake tasted delicious and my husband was very happy. He was so touched by our efforts that I realized how silly I had been. What if none of us ever sang, because we might not be Pavarotti? Should we all give up running, in the firm knowledge that Usain Bolt would always be faster? My cake was nothing like Fanny's, but the chocolate and the love were there, and I think she would have been proud.

Fanny's Chocolate Cream Cheese Layer Cake

11 oz. cream cheese (room temperature)
2 boxes powdered sugar
2 sticks margarine (room temperature)
2 tablespoons cocoa
6 oz. chocolate bits or chips
¼ cup hot water

Melt both kinds of chocolate in hot water.
Mix with other ingredients.
Divide half out and save for icing.

2 ½ cup plain flour
3 eggs
1 teaspoon soda
1 teaspoon salt
1 cup buttermilk
1 teaspoon vanilla

Mix together all but the flour.
Add half of cream cheese mixture.
Add all to flour.
Pour batter in three 9" or four 8" wax paper lined pans.
Beat in pans to remove bubbles.
Cook thirty minutes at 350°.
Cool and ice.

Beatrice's Chicken and Dumplings
Jayne Padgett Bowers

My grandmother, Beatrice Emmaline Smart Padgett, made the best chicken and dumplings in the world. No exaggeration. And her Angel Biscuits were to die for! When I later remarked on what an excellent cook my grandmother was, my aunt Polly told me that when her mother was a child, all of the children had specific jobs to carry out. My grandmother Beatrice was assigned to the kitchen.

Her chicken and dumplings remain unsurpassed to this day, even by the likes of Paula Deen. When I was a newlywed, I tried to duplicate her recipe with disastrous results. I had carefully written down her verbal instructions, including a pinch of this and spoonful of that, and felt confident that my culinary concoction would be scrumptious.

As soon as I dropped the carefully rolled out and neatly cut flour strips in the boiling liquid, I knew something was wrong. The color just didn't look right—too blah. The dumplings plumped up like hers did, but as we soon discovered, they were tasteless and lacked the thick creaminess of my grandmother's.

When I recounted my steps for her, my grandmother looked puzzled for a few moments and then asked me about the liquid. Had I used both dark and white pieces of chicken to make the broth or just white? White meat was drier, she said, and not as tasty. Broth? She hadn't said anything about broth, just "liquid." A novice cook, I had used good old water for my liquid and Swanson's canned chicken for the meat.

I can still hear my grandmother's lively cackle as she threw back her head and had a good laugh at my expense. After a few moments, she recovered her composure and then added a few more specific instructions to her recipe.

Chicken and Dumplings

For the broth:
1 chicken, cut into pieces
2 chicken bouillon cubes
Salt and pepper to taste

Place chicken in pot and cover well with water. Put on lid and simmer until tender, about one or two hours, depending on whether it is an older hen or a year old chicken. Remove lid for last half hour of cooking. Add canned broth or another bouillon cube and water so you have about four cups of good, strong liquid. Take chicken out of broth. Dip out 1/2 cup of broth to use for dumplings.

When chicken is cool, remove from bones and set aside.

For the dumplings:

2 to 2 ½ cups all-purpose flour
I teaspoon salt
Take ½ cup of previously reserved broth with enough ice cubes to make 1 cup total of broth.

Mix salt into flour and put in mixing bowl. Add cold broth slowly in center and knead into a stiff dough. Place on well-floured surface and roll out with floured rolling pin until very thin, no more than 1/8 inch. Cut into inch strips and let rest for ten minutes.

Bring broth to boil.

Drop the dumplings into the boiling broth one at a time, allowing boil to return before adding another dumpling strip. Once all the dumplings are in the broth, add chicken, stir once and put on a lid. Cook on medium heat for about 10 to 12 minutes, until the broth thickens. Add more salt and pepper if needed and let sit a few minutes for flavors to mingle.

RECIPES FROM A VINTAGE COOKBOOK

Soup for an Invalid

One pint sweet milk
One egg
One teaspoon butter
Two teaspoons flour that has been browned in skillet

Take out about a gill of milk and put the rest on to boil in a granite saucepan. Beat the egg and put it into the flour. Stir until smooth. Put in cold milk and stir until smooth once again. When the other milk is boiling, pour this flour and cold milk mix in very slowly. Put in butter and season with a little bit of salt and pepper if the stomach can stand it. Cook until thick as thick cream.

(A gill is an old measuring unit equal to about ¼ of a pint.)

Blackberry Wine

To four quarts of berries, add one quart of boiling water. Let it stand for a full day and night. Strain. To every gallon of juice add 3½ pounds sugar.

Let it stand for two months. It is then fit for use,

Filter your wine through clean cotton.

Six quarts of berries make around one gallon of juice.

SAUERKRAUT RECIPE FROM AN OLD COOKBOOK

Printed as written

For five gallon jug, 50 # cabbage

Use large outside leaves to line crock. Start by covering bottom & add sides as layers used.

Core cabbage. Quarter and shred as fine as possible.

Put in 2" layers with 1/3 cup coarse salt. Use potato masher to break cabbage while packing. Pack hard. Do not splash brine-it will damage floor.

When full, wrap platter in cloth & hold cabbage under brine. Use washed brick on plate.

Place in cool place out of sun. Leave six weeks. If brine runs over, wipe sides. If not enough to cover cabbage add salted water (2 teaspoons per quart).

When over fermenting remove 1 inch and feed to the birds. Put the rest in jar with paraffin and store.

BETTIE'S BUTTERED & ROASTED PECANS
Martha Dabbs Greenway

1 pound pecans
1 stick of butter
Salt

Preheat oven to 250-275 degrees.

Spread nuts on cookie sheet, single layer. Cut up one stick of butter over nuts and sprinkle liberally with salt.

Set timer for every ten minutes and stir, flip nuts and salt again. Do this 3-4 times depending on your oven. Color will change as they cook. Cook until they taste "right."

Made each Christmas and sometimes at Thanksgiving.

Cheese Biscuits from the Quaker Café
Brenda Bevan Remmes

Dump in a bowl:
2 cups self-rising flour
1 stick of cold butter cut into 8 chunks
1 cup sharp cheddar cheese grated
a pinch of red pepper

With your hands rub it all together until everything is crumble size.
That means don't stir or mix!

Make hole in the middle of the mixture and pour in
¾ cups of cream – maybe more
(You can substitute milk if you're on a diet but if you're planning on eating biscuits, you shouldn't be thinking diet anyway).

With a big spoon or your hand swoop around the bowl no more than 4-5 times.
You should have a moist mixture (too moist for rolling out).

Dump it all on a generously floured surface.
Dust more flour on top so you can pat it out.
Pat down with hands to about ½ inch thick

Cut with small biscuit cutter no bigger than a fifty-cent piece.
Place on greased or non-stick cookie sheet.

Bake in 450 oven for 10-15 min.
Watch bottoms so they don't burn.

Serve hot and My-oh-My!

If they're any left over (unlikely), slice them for the next meal, add a smidgen of butter and toast under the broiler.

THE STANDING PEOPLE

My first copies of Treasure Island and Huckleberry Finn still have some blue spruce needles scattered in the pages. They smell of Christmas still.

Charlton Heston

Camden Writers

The Standing People
Lauren Allen

The landscape has changed since my childhood. We used to roam all over the countryside, riding horses and playing Indian, and all year round we kept an eye out for the perfect Christmas tree. Now many acres of loblolly and longleaf pines are gone, cut down and hauled off with giant, raucous machines, leaving a sad stubble behind. But the old gnarled witness tree still stands sentry at the trailhead, a blue slash of paint marking its trunk for passover even though the surveyors have

planted white plastic posts into the ground to more accurately mark the property line.

Trees tend to shadow our lives in ways it is easy to overlook. My mother's constant warning when we were kids was "Don't go past the oak tree"—the boundary beyond which we were inexplicably unsafe. Maybe my memory reveals the incomplete understanding of a child, but I don't recall property lines being so vigilantly guarded by anyone other than the "standing people" (as Native Americans used to reverently refer to trees). Now wooden fences belligerently block the way and trees bear signs that threaten prosecution.

Our definition of the perfect Christmas tree was relative. It was usually a young longleaf pine that was fairly straight and full, it had to have a good clean top for the tree-topper angel that held the star, and needed lots of branches to hang my mother's extensive handmade ornament collection. The fragile stars alone, tatted and starched by my grandmother, could have decorated the whole tree by themselves, but they were accompanied by tiny blown eggs, intricate little figures tucked into walnut shells, carved wooden angels, and teensy embroidered manger scenes.

Harvesting the Christmas tree meant a hike out with Dad to locate it, and if it passed muster, cut it down and drag it home. In the house it usually looked scrawny and bald, and we had to twist and turn it to hide the gaping holes in the branches. Dad would insert shims underneath to hide the lean, but once it was loaded with lights and ornaments it was magical.

We were not very religious most of the year, but when family and friends gathered around the tree and the time came for Christmas dinner, everyone stood around the dining room table and my father said a blessing. Our dining room table used to be a chopping block in a warehouse—in fact much of the house is reclaimed wood from an old freezer locker building: some of the floors are transplanted and the walls are oak salvaged from pallets that were stacked inside. One year, before he became sick with cancer and before we were aware of his impending absence, he said grace about the gift of *presence*. He had a catch in his voice as he embroidered a pun: *presents* under the tree, the past carried into the *present*, and his prayer encouraged the sort of intelligent and careful consciousness of one who is mindful and grateful.

The smell of pine shavings or sawdust still summons my father instantly. He worked on renovating many of the old plantation homes in Camden and surrounding areas, always imaginatively bridging the past and the present, honoring the aging beauty of the grand wooden mansions but seeking to square them with the times and protect them for the future. I imagine he was aware of how much trees gave to him, from the wood that he sawed and hammered on a daily basis to fit the needs at hand, to the pages of the philosophy books he loved to read— even the tiny pencil stub he always tucked behind his ear to mark boards with and to scratch notes.

Things have changed. This land was farmed by my mother's grandfather, but its history stretches back much farther than his story. Our dirt road curves all the way back through the years to early

America when it was part of a British supply line during the Revolutionary War. Occasionally stone spear points turn up in the horse pasture, predating even the birth of Christ.

Nowadays we have given up the Christmas tree hunt—like everyone else, we drive to the tree stand that sprouts overnight near the grocery store somewhere around Thanksgiving and buy a too-perfect tree to celebrate the holidays.

We still drive it home and stand it in the same living room in the house my father built, one of the first and best things he made.

Our roots go deep here.

The Allen Sisters

Stop Singing
Martha Dabbs Greenway

It wouldn't have been so bad if I'd not spent my last dollar at the lottery window. To be poor is not bad but to spend money poorly is not good.

It was almost Christmas and the dark night began early. I knew the neighborhood children would soon come by to sing carols and collect money for the Children's Hospital. "Damn," I muttered as I went to the back of the house. "Why didn't I save at least a few coins for them?"

Newly married and almost always broke, my husband and I lived in a small cabin perched down the hill from the street and close to the small stream that ran through the neighborhood. He was out of town at a sales meeting. I turned the lights out in the front room and settled under the dim overhead light of the kitchen where the old Royal manual typewriter waited for me. I had reports I'd promised to do. I soon forgot about the children.

I heard a knock on the door. Three soft taps.

Without thinking, I walked through the dark front room, switched on the porch light and opened the door.

There they stood: two little ones—a boy about four and a beautiful little girl about three. Two chaperones stayed back in the shadows and the rest of the group remained on the street . . . . the sweet carols wafting down past me and into my house.

"Hello," said the boy. "We're collecting money for the Children's Hospital."

Leaning closer, I thanked him for what they were doing but explained that I had no money.

Upon hearing this, the boy turned to the group and shouted, "Stop singing!"

The little girl chimed in, "She doesn't have any money!"

The chaperones tried to stifle their chuckles and the choir on the street fell into a stunned silence—my just reward for spending that last dollar on a gamble instead of a song.

"Little Christmas"
Paddy Bell

"Little Christmas," also known as the Feast of Saint Nicholas, falls on December 6th right on the heels of Thanksgiving. It signals the absolute final safe date to finish off any left-over cranberry relish or turkey hash still in the fridge, and for my family, it serves as the official kick-off to the Christmas season.

Saint Nicholas - not to be confused with Clement Moore's St. Nick, that right jolly old elf, was a 4th Century Christian bishop in ancient Myra, Turkey. He devoted his life to serving the needy, the hungry, the poor, and the underprivileged. He is revered as the patron saint of an oddly assorted group, which includes sailors, students, merchants, children, and of all things, repentant thieves! Legend holds that Saint Nicholas gifted in secrecy. He made charitable rounds in the darkness of night, leaving food, coins, and little treasures on doorsteps, down chimneys, and even in shoes left on a threshold. His faithful traveling companion, assistant, and protector was Knecht Ruprecht, translated, Knight Rupert.

This pair set out together every December 6th eve to visit homes and secretly leave rewards for the nice…or reminders for the naughty to shape up before the Big Christmas, just nineteen days away. In my childhood, I thought of Rupert as a bad cop who delivered switches and lumps of coal to mischievous and ill-mannered children – the antithesis of good cop Nicholas, who brought candy, fruit, nuts, gingerbread, and small toys for the virtuous.

As far back as memory serves, my parents, two brothers and I spent every "Little Christmas" at the home of family friends, the Joneses. Seven anxious kids, four parents, and a number of other relatives gathered for the evening supper, which was hastily wolfed down to get on to the watching and waiting for the arrival of the Holy Saint.

The Jones' home was a mid-century 1950's version of a split-level. The front door opened to steps that led down to a subterranean living room with ground-level windows. All were gathered there, adults happily chatting away, sipping on drinks or coffee. The children toyed at amusement, but kept eyes focused on that front door as we waited with a combination of excitement and trepidation.

"Rupert's got you on his bad list," the oldest Jones boy teased me.

"Does not."

"Does too."

I frantically reviewed the year's behaviors and misbehaviors, and felt confident that Saint Nicholas would remember me well. Yet there was always a smidgen of worry that Rupert might convince the Saint otherwise.

I still retorted with another "Does not!"

RAP-TAP-A-TAP on the window.

I raced to the farthest corner of the room, my eyes glued to the door. We shrieked and giggled and chorused, "Yea! It's St. Nicholas! He's here! He's here!"

Under my breath I whispered, "But so is Rupert. He's here too!"

KNOCK KNOCK on the door.

SWOOSH!

The door blew open, admitting a blast of wintry air and a billow of powdery snow. A bundle of sticks thudded down the stairs, clearly announcing that Rupert was out there.

Dread-filled seconds of silence and emptiness followed as we gaped in wonder at the dark hole at the top of the stairs and the swirling snow.

Was this it? Would this be the year our beloved Saint Nicholas forgot us? Would it just be switches and sticks?

Then in a flurry, seven brown paper packages tied up in twine tumbled down the steps. The door slammed shut – all in a matter of seconds. Six children pounced on the pile to claim their own loot. Names were printed in neat block caps on the bags. My brother retrieved my stash, aware that Mom already had me in the bathroom to change my britches. Oh yes, Rupert once again scared the pee out of me. Every year, always the same.

Perhaps it was too much grape juice, a guilty conscience, or the over-active imagination of a future fiction writer that made Rupert more to me than Nicholas's friend and guardian. As years passed, the emphasis of "Little Christmas" shifted to the lesson of the revered

Saint and his good works, and less on his chum Rupert. In the Catholic
College I attended, students placed their shoes in the dorm hallway at
lights-out on December 6th eve. The next morning, we found them
filled with fruit, candy, nuts, a quarter or two, and a Holy Card
featuring a colorful picture of Nicholas, the benevolent bishop and
patron saint of children.

Sadly, I've turned loose the "Little Christmas" traditions, but
still fondly recall those many feast days spent with family and friends.
The gifts of coloring books, crayons, jump ropes, balsa airplanes, and
Silly Putty eggs tucked into paper bags with oranges, candies, and nuts
are long gone. But I still have the Holy Card from my college days,
and when I recite the prayer to Saint Nicholas, I fondly remember his
faithful sidekick, and for good measure, throw in a prayer to Rupert as
well.

Man, Was I Wrong
Nick West

In 1947, at the tender age five, my best friend and I were playing ball in the yard.

"You do know that Santa Claus isn't real?" Bob said.

"What do you mean, Santa's not real?" I asked.

"Your parents buy all the toys you get at Christmas."

"Can't be," I said with all the authority I could muster. "They don't have that much money."

"Well, it's the truth, there is no Santa Claus."

In 1947, I realized that Bob was a lot smarter than me. Even in kindergarten, he knew more cool stuff than anyone else. Most anything he told me I believed to be the whole truth, and when he said there was no Santa Claus, I took it to heart.

I dared not ask my mom if it were true. I was clever or devious enough to conceal many things from my parents. If Bob was right and my parents found out I knew about Santa, I worried the toys might go away. I feared that there might never be another Christmas.

As the holiday approached, the thought of no Santa Claus consumed me. *What other lies had my parents told me,* I wondered. *How would I ever fully know what was true and what was a lie? If I couldn't trust my parents, who could I trust?*

If there wasn't a Santa Claus, I could see the sad end of Christmas for me and my four-year-old brother.

Finally, the holiday was upon us. We left home to spend Christmas Eve night with my grandparents in Kershaw. There was great excitement, but I felt my own anxiety building.

As my brother and I climbed in our two single beds that night, neither of us could go to sleep. Except for a thin shaft of light sliding in under the door, the room was completely dark. There in the silence, I thought back over what my friend had told me. Fearful that he might go to our mother with Bob's poisonous message, I had not shared with my brother the possibility that this part of Christmas, with presents magically appearing and stockings stuffed to overflowing, was no more than a game. I felt alone and torn between two worlds: one was with Santa Claus; the other without him. The idea that Bob might know the truth made my insides jittery looked out the window one last time. It had begun to snow, something of a little miracle itself in the deep South. I got back in bed finally, and sleep crept over me. Next thing I knew it was nearly morning.

My brother and I went to wake Mom and Dad, and then, just as everyone began to gather and wish each other Merry Christmas, a loud rumbling noise shook the entire house. We all ran outside in bedroom shoes, the cold wind slapping at our bathrobes. We looked up to where the yellow streetlight shone on the top of the house. The chimney had fallen! Red bricks lay scattered on the roof and on the snow-covered ground.

My Grandma, seemingly unperturbed, patted me on the head. "Nick," she said, "I guess Santa knocked the chimney down getting out tonight."

At that moment I knew there really was a Santa Claus after all. Grandma had saved the day.

Later that day I saw Bob, and I told him about the chimney falling at Grandma's, I told him what Grandma said. We were both elated that there was a real Santa Claus after all. That terrible gut feeling that had been eating me alive had vanished.

As we walked along, Bob, who would one day become a scientist with N.A.S.A., shook his head in disbelief. "Man, he said, "was I ever wrong."

My Father's Christmas
Brenda Bevan Remmes

My father loved Christmas more than any person I know. He told us when he was a boy growing up in a strict Methodist family in Pennsylvania, he and his three brothers received a basket of fruit and nuts under the tree—the sum total of the gift-giving.

My father and his brothers all became men of substance: important men, busy men, men addicted to proving themselves by putting in long hours at their jobs at the expense of time with their families. Christmas turned into my father's moment to give back for all the violin concerts, baseball games and little theater performances he'd missed.

What my father bestowed upon us came in waves, an excess of curiosities depending on the best deal that caught his eye during the few times he walked through the local department store. In an effort, I think, not to offend or show favoritism, he often gave us all the same thing. With the advent of 24-hour specials sandwiched in between the occasional television shows he watched, his gifts became amusingly predictable.

I recall Christmases where we all got a suitcase, pillows, or a steak knife set. Remember those little orange plastic skewers to core an apple? We got those along with an onion slicer specially designed to make fried onion rings, comical since none of us liked onion rings.

Only later did I realize my mother *loved* onion rings, but refrained from cooking anything fried.

We received make-up kits, even though we wore little make-up, and numerous boxes of dusting powder, which we stacked in closets between chocolate covered cherries wrapped in silver foil. At one point he developed a friendship with a fine jewelry dealer. That was a banner year. Alas, the dealer died shortly thereafter and that was the end of what we all hoped would be a new standard of gifts that might appear under the tree.

My father's generosity extended far beyond our immediate family. It was a rare person who knew him that didn't receive a seasonal token of appreciation. As he approached what he knew would be his last Christmas, he went into a frenzy of catalog buying. Some days the UPS and FedEx trucks sat bumper to bumper in his drive waiting their turn to unload. Mother would simply roll her eyes and disappear into the kitchen as the packages piled up. After his death, she overheard several women at her beauty parlor discussing the wonderful shortbread cookies he had sent them for Christmas. My mother had never met the women and didn't introduce herself, but she paid the credit card bill for two-dozen orders.

Last Christmas as I sat around the lit tree with my boys and their families, we began to reminisce about the gifts they'd received from me in the past. "Remember the year you gave us luggage?" my youngest asked. "What were we, eight and ten? Were you trying to get rid of us?"

"Did I give you luggage?" I asked. "Surely not."

"Yep, and then there was the year you gave us pillows," the oldest said. "We got *pillows* from Santa Claus. I couldn't believe it. My friends laughed out loud."

"Pillows I remember," I confessed. "They were goose down—on sale—a rare find. You slept better, didn't you?"

"What about those crystal balls from Czechoslovakia?"

"I thought they might be valuable someday," I said. "A friend gave me a deal."

"And the country western CDs of Charlie Pride? Really, Mom."

I slumped in my chair. "That bad, huh?"

"It was pretty weird," one said and the other nodded in agreement. "We just figured you went a little bonkers around Christmas time. We gave up telling you what we wanted and decided aliens from outer space took control of your mind."

"I suppose," I admitted. "But, honestly," I paused and threw up my arms in a small gesture of apology. "It seemed perfectly acceptable at the time."

Christmas Cookies at Easter
Vanessa Friedrich

As a child in my grandmother's house in Germany, my sister Jenna and I looked forward every holiday season to baking Christmas cookies with Oma, that's how we called our grandmother. Oma made the dough and Jenna and I cut out cookies using all sorts of different forms. We used hearts, stars, and angel forms which all looked like they were used by Oma's grandmother.

With the angels, we always had to be extra careful not to cut a wing or an arm off when we lifted them up off the table and into the oven. For that reason, I always preferred the heart form or, even better, the simple circle forms, which were a lot easier to cut out without messing up. While doing all this, we never missed the opportunity to try some of the heavenly sweet dough with our fingers.

Oma made different types of delicious dough. We had a dark brown chocolate one, a light colored sugared one, the gooey one for the honey cake, and a special dark one for the thick cookie hearts. For some reason, the special dark dough never tasted as sweet unbaked as the others. Our favorite was the light colored sugared dough that we loved to lick off the spoon just like that.

After the cookies were baked, the thick dark hearts came out of the oven perfectly formed but hard as rock. After they cooled down we glazed them with chocolate syrup and, as the last touch up for looks, put colorful sprinkles on top.

We could never bear to wait until Christmas but started digging into them as soon as they were done. The only cookie to safely last until Christmas was the chocolate heart cookies, because they were way too hard to eat. For the next weeks, the hearts stayed that way and one would run the risk of breaking a tooth by trying to eat them.

"Leave them alone until they soften up," Oma would warn us. It always turned out to be months before the chocolate hearts became edible.

Every year, there we were again at Easter, and then we could enjoy the cookies we made for Christmas. They not only tasted good on Easter, but they also provided good entertainment to everybody who heard about our special cookie hearts, which took all winter to become enjoyable.

Best and Worst Christmases
Nick West

Christmas disappointments and heartbreaks occur, and for this reason, many people are diagnosed with depression during the holiday season. Every Christmas becomes a painful reminder of a sorrow suffered, no matter how far back in the past.

Long ago three women had their best and worst Christmases: Annie is now 101 years old, Betty is 91 years old, and last year, Jennie died at the age of 98. Annie and Betty are currently residents at The Methodist Manor in Florence and are friends of my 93-year-old mother.

Annie had turned four years old when she had her best and worst Christmas. Her family lived meagerly, but she and her brother Sam were loved dearly by their parents.

Christmas in their home meant just one toy, one piece of clothing and some fruit, but 1917 was different. Annie received her first doll. She had blond hair, clear blue eyes, and a face without blemish.

Annie carried this precious gift everywhere she went this Christmas day. But just before supper, as she rounded the corner in the kitchen, Sam ran straight into her. The doll dropped from her arms to the heart pine flooring. The bisque face shattered into many small pieces.

She remembers how she screamed in horror.

Annie's mother attempted to console her, but to no avail. Her father told her he might be able to repair it.

Annie wasn't able to eat supper, and when she went to bed, she was still sobbing.

Later that night, her dad did attempt to fix the doll, but after several hours, he realized it was impossible. The next morning her father gave her the bad news, and she went by the trashcan in the kitchen, she saw the pitiful remains of her doll. This was the Christmas, she says, that started out to be her best Christmas ever, but ended being her worst.

***

Betty's best and worst Christmas came at the age of 4. Her brother Jim had recently turned 9.

Like Annie, she received a doll. Hers had auburn hair and green eyes with stuffed cloth arms, legs, and neck. In her mind, it was exquisite.

Betty exuded pride of her new doll and the additional clothes that came with it. She carried it to her room where she changed clothes and shoes for several hours. But after Christmas dinner, she felt tired and fell asleep on the sofa. They had gotten up early that morning, and now she took a long nap.

An hour and a half later, she walked into her bedroom and found her brother standing over her doll with a large knife. For Christmas, Jim had received a doctor's bag with stethoscope and so many other medical items, he must have imagined himself a surgeon.

He had operated on the doll with a butcher knife, removing both the legs and arms of the new doll.

Betty shrill scream pierced through the house, and her mother and father came running.

Jim got the only spanking he ever received on a Christmas day.

That afternoon Betty's mom sewed the arms and legs back on the doll. Betty put the doll on a shelf and never played with it again And although Jim did become a medical doctor, to this day, he has never performed any other surgery.

***

Jennie, raised by a wealthy southern family, attended the University of Virginia in Charlottesville. While a student there, she befriended a young man from Richmond. They courted for two years and became serious enough to plan on marriage once they graduated.

But prior to graduation, World War II broke out and Rhett enlisted in the military. He had only two weeks before he would have to leave and Rhett wanted to marry immediately. But Jennie said no. When he got back if he still wanted to marry her, she told him, she would accept.

Still a single man, Rhett left on a train for Fort Jackson. Within a few short months, he found himself in Europe in the middle of the fight.

Over the next year and a half, Jennie and Rhett wrote many letters to one another. The long separation seemed to have strengthened their love.

In the autumn of 1943, Rhett wrote with good news: he hoped to be home for Christmas.

Jennie waited for the next three months as the holidays approached. Finally, Rhett wrote that he would be arriving in New York City on Christmas day. "Would you come meet me?" he asked.

She wrote his mother and father and invited them to accompany her.

Four days before Christmas, a visitor came to the University of Virginia and asked to see Miss Jennie Scott. As soon as she saw Rhett's father, tears running down his cheek, she knew. He handed her the telegram he had received that morning. Rhett had been killed two days earlier.

When Jennie turned 94, her nephew asked her about a stack of letters he found in some of her possessions that were stored in the attic.

"Do they have a blue ribbon around them?"

"Yes," he replied.

She told him about Rhett, and about how much she loved him. She knew there would never be another man for her, she said.

She asked her nephew if he would please burn the letters.

Reluctantly, he carried out Jennie's request. He took the stack of letters, loosed them from their ribbon, and watched as, one by one, they blazed up in the fireplace before they curled to ash.

Candy Bells and Brazil Nuts

Jayne Padgett Bowers

What, I wondered, was Mrs. Bowers thinking as she listened to her great grandchildren exclaim over their Christmas gifts? So much gaiety and excitement! Such anticipation for what the next gift would be. So little patience for when it would be "My turn, my turn!"

According to stories I'd heard, the raucous scene in front of the Christmas tree at our home was radically different from the ones of her childhood. Back then there had been only one celebration, not the several that these little ones would experience over a two or three week period. And gifts? This ripping and tearing of beautiful paper would take place numerous times during the Christmas season, but for her and her siblings, gifts had been meager in the 1920's and 30's.

Her reflections of Christmases past revealed little similarity to the one her children, grandchildren, and great grandchildren celebrated in 2013. How can an orange and a cloth doll compare to culinary concoctions galore and a Kindle Fire? How can an unlit, sparsely decorated tree of her childhood compare to a pre-lit Christmas tree shining brightly in the foyer, its small gumdrop lights casting a glow on the russet red walls?

What a difference 80 years makes! Curious about her childhood Christmases, I asked Mrs. Bowers to describe one for me.

"Back then," she began, "Papa would go to the woods with a couple or three of us and pick out a tree. He'd cut it down and drag it home. Before he'd bring it in the house, he'd cut it off and nail it to a block."

"Did you and your sisters string popcorn or put candy canes on it?" I asked.

With a chuckle, she replied, "No, we had never tasted any popcorn, much less string it for a tree. Our decorations were more simple than that."

As I wondered what could be simpler than popcorn, Mrs. Bowers began to describe the Greene family Christmas tree. For starters, she and her siblings, seven sisters and two brothers, threw pieces of cotton on it for a snowy effect.

"Pieces of cotton?" I asked.

"You know, cotton bolls that we got from the fields."

Then the children got creative. Using pieces of paper from the orange and tangerine crates sent from Uncle Arthur in Florida, the sisters cut colorful strips to hang on the freshly cut, fragrant tree.

Uncle Arthur had moved to sunny Florida decades before, and every December he sent two wooden crates of fruit, one of oranges and one of tangerines, to the family. The citrusy smell was divine, and the tangy taste was even better. Years later, Mrs. Bowers remembers the sweetness of the tangerines compared to the tartness of the oranges. The oranges were so juicy that she and her sisters and brothers always had sticky fingers and forearms as the rich juice oozed out of the fruit and onto their skin. The tangerines were smaller, easier to peel, and neater to eat.

There were other tasty seasonal treats in the Greene home. "Papa always went to town and got nuts and candy," she told me.

I prodded. "What kind?"

"No chocolate. The candy was jelly-like and in the shape of bells. The outside was sugar coated, not slick. There were different colors too."

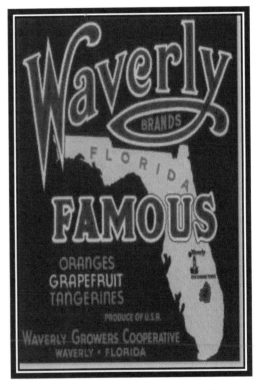

"Like what?" I asked. "Red and green for Christmas? "

"Well yeah, but orange and yellow too. I liked it. It was chewy and stuck to the top of my mouth and teeth like glue, but I still liked it."

She added, "Papa always brought home some candy sticks too, with stripes around them."

"What about the nuts? Did he buy a box of mixed nuts?"

"No, just two kinds. A box of Brazil nuts and one of English walnuts."

I wanted to know about Christmas day. Was there a huge meal? Did relatives come from neighboring towns? Did the family spend the morning enjoying their gifts? Did they sing? Did someone read the Christmas story from the Bible?

"Papa always made sure everyone had a shoebox, box lid, or pie pan with their Christmas goodies in it. I usually got a cloth doll and some fruit in mine."

One year she noticed that Santa's handwriting was amazingly like her father's and gleefully told him, "Papa, Santa Claus writes just like you, kind of fancy." She laughs at the memory, remembering her naïve innocence.

There was always a big Christmas dinner with the usual holiday fare: a hen, dressing, dumplings, peas, beans, biscuits, and cakes and pies galore. Her mother made cakes and pies during the week leading up to the big day. There were coconut, chocolate, and raisin cakes and chocolate, coconut, and apple pies. Since aunts, uncles, and grandparents lived a good distance away, it was usually just the immediate family who shared the holiday meal.

"Was this the way your family celebrated every year?" I asked.

"Pretty much. But things changed somewhat as we got older. We could help out more with the preparations."

One year, her sister Jane was allowed to go Christmas shopping with her mother. Two years older than Mrs. Bowers (little Willie), the two sisters were quite close and shared all sorts of confidences. Unfortunately, this time Jane went too far with secret sharing, and when they came in from shopping, she unknowingly ruined that year's Christmas for her younger sister.

Jane coaxed her out to the barn beyond hearing distance of the others and preceded to tell Willie everything their mother had bought for the family. Everything. There in the mule stable in the barn, excitement turned to distress, anticipation to sadness.

Years passed, and the Greene children married and had families of their own. Yet, each December they gather to celebrate their strong family bond and to reminisce about the Christmases of yesteryear, the kind of Christmases we all long for, the ones based on togetherness and love.

Although they can afford elaborate gifts and expensive food, they prefer to keep it simple. The gifts are small ones to be awarded to Bingo winners. The food is predictable but delicious with each person bringing his or her specialty. They laugh, play games, sing carols, and remember Papa's gifts, Mama's chocolate cake, and Uncle Arthur's juicy oranges.

Protecting Mommy
Paddy Bell

Five or six
    Way too young
        Questioning his Dad

Santa Claus?
    North Pole home?
        Lists of good and bad?

Mrs. Claus?
    Elves make toys?
        Reindeer take to flight?

Round the world?
    Magic sleigh?
        All in just one night?

Let's pretend
    It's all true
        On this Christmas eve

Hang our socks
    Play along
        Mommy still believes.

The exact words that my son, Ryan, said to his Dad those many years ago were:

"Hey, Dad, I'm pretty sure that flying reindeer story around the whole big world in one night can't be true. But we have to be real careful around Mommy, because she still believes."

Ryan, now 44, has children of his own who believe with all their hearts.

Pumpkins In Shadows
Mindy Blakely

*Sung to the tune of "My Favorite Things"

Pumpkins in shadows and ghosts in the trees,
Eerie screams echoing in the slight breeze,
Brown paper bags holding candles inside,
Many dark places for monsters to hide.

When the owl hoots,
When the bat flies,
When Frankenstein starts to rise,
I leap to my feet and run fast as can be,
So that I won't feel terrorized!

Real haunted houses with spiders and mice,
Flashlights that flicker once and then twice,
Scary piano music that plays by itself,
Cobwebs and creatures crawling on shelves.

When the owl hoots,
When the bat flies,
When Frankenstein starts to rise,
I leap to my feet and run fast as can be,
so that I won't feel terrorized!

Witches and Goblins and spooks fill the street,
Children in doorways for a trick or a treat,
Faces in makeup, but can you guess who?
Lights go out just when somebody yells, **"*Boo!*"**

When the owl hoots,
When the bat flies,
When Frankenstein starts to rise,
I leap to my feet and run fast as can be
So that I won't feel terrorized!

Storms full of lightning and thunder that rings,
Corpses in graveyards and insects with wings,
Werewolves and vampires in blood that still clings,
These are a few very frightening things.

When the owl hoots,
When the bat flies,
When I'm feeling scared,
I try to forget my foolish nightmares,
Demons can't hurt me; nobody else dares.

When the owl hoots,
When the bat flies,
When Frankenstein starts to rise,
I leap to my feet and run fast as can be,
So that I won't feel *Terrorized!!*

WE AND THE LAND ARE ONE

I bequeath myself to the dirt to grow from the grass I love. If you want me again, look for me under your bootsoles.

Walt Whitman, *Leaves of Grass*

WE AND THE LAND ARE ONE
Jayne Bowers

Carrying on the family farming tradition, HOFIELD Farms officially opened for business on a foggy spring morning in 1980. Chuckling as he remembered that day, my cousin Robert said, "We gave people strawberry baskets and pointed to the fields. You couldn't even see them because the fog was so heavy and low that day, but the people went out anyway. It was weird seeing them get sort of swallowed up by that fog."

Before HOFIELD, an acronym for Hope, Opportunity, Faith, Integrity, Energy, Land, and Determination, became something of a Camden institution, the Marsh and Mickle families were well known throughout the farming community. My aunt, Polly Padgett Marsh, wrote that being a farmer was not an easy thing to do "UNLESS a young man is born into a farm family, inherited a bundle or money, or finds a mentor farmer who has no family to pass his farm to....Bob had generations of farmers in his past on both sides."

Fortunately, Polly wrote many of her memories of those early days. A young wife and mother, here's Polly's recollection of her first visit to the tobacco market. The year was 1954, and the location was Lake City. It's wonderful to imagine her reactions to the noisy hustle and bustle of the place, especially the constant chant of the auctioneer, as she and her young son Robert visited the warehouse that August morning.

It was that same summer I went to my first tobacco market. Bob loaded the big truck after dark and drove to the market early enough to get our tobacco on the floor before the auction started. Bub drove me and Robert down the next morning. I was not prepared for the number of people or the amount of tobacco on the floor. It was laid out in rows of stacked tobacco, some two sheets high. And the noise!

But the thing I remember most was the smell. It was more of a fragrance to me. I had always enjoyed the smell of a pipe or cigar, so to me it was a pleasant smell. Many years later I heard a woman working with her family's tobacco say that she liked the smell—to her it smelled like money. I met a small grower selling his crop that morning. He was enjoying smoking a cigar and told me that was the only time he could afford to smoke, when the money was coming in.

The auctioneer would walk down between the piles of tobacco with the buyers following and the farmers coming behind, watching for the crop to be sold. A warehouse employee was behind the auctioneer, carrying a clipboard and writing all the time, leaving paperwork on each pile that was sold. Sometimes a pile would not sell due to moisture or color. A producer had the option to refuse a sale if he did not find it acceptable. He had several options but whatever was decided, he could go home that night with a check in his pocket.

Polly became increasingly involved with the farm, and she writes of a typical fall day when Robert, her oldest child, was a year old. Already busy, she probably couldn't envision a day with six children and the endless cycle of cooking, laundry, cleaning, and learning that a large family would entail.

Bob would get up at three o'clock to get ready for the day. He would drive to town and make a circle picking up cotton pickers. About 11:00 I put Robert in the car and would get my legal pad and go to the field. The pickers didn't bring lunch so I took orders. There were no fast food restaurants so we went to the little country store. A little cheese, a little baloney, a honey bun and a Pepsi or an RC cola. The pickers didn't bring any money, so I kept a record of each one and delivered their lunch back to the field.

At the end of the day, Robert and I went back to the field with my legal pad to record the cotton weights. The cotton was tied up in burlap sheets and weighed. Sheets were stacked on a trailer or truck for the trip to the gin. Bob would take the pickers back to town. It made for a very long day.

As the family grew, Polly and Bob wrestled with the question of whether it was better to spend the money on the farm or on the home. With four children, two of them twin babies, Polly asked for an up-to-date washing machine to replace the ringer washer that hooked up to the kitchen sink, but Bob said they couldn't afford it. They were at an impasse, and something had to give. The following excerpt from Polly's journal is actually one of the family stories that all of children and grandchildren know about. Cynthia, the second daughter, believes it's because what happened was so out of character for her mother.

One June day I went to town grocery buying, taking the two older children with me and leaving the twins with Ruth, a young colored woman who was helping a couple of days a week. It was hot and I still thought you had to dress to go to town, so I was wearing two-inch heels.

Arriving back home at lunch time, bringing in a week's groceries and with two hungry children and two hungry babies waiting, the washing machine was still hooked up to the faucet making the sink inaccessible. While trying to decide on a course of action, Bob came bouncing in, all excited. He said, Guess what? We now own a combine."

Acting on impulse, I took off my heels and threw them at him across the 20 foot room. That was the first and last time I ever threw anything. Needless to say, that afternoon we drove to Sears in Columbia and came home with a repossessed washing machine. It was another ten years before we bought a dryer. I found it ironic that when the twins married, they both had new washers and dryers installed while they were on their honeymoon.

The six Marsh children all love the land. The youngest, Sue Marsh Hardin felt such a loyalty that she was married at HOFIELD on May 8, 1988. It was a 6:00 o'clock a.m. wedding, one that I'll always remember. The minister pronounced them husband and wife at the exact moment when the sun rose from the horizon like a huge ball.

SUNRISE WEDDING AT HOFIELD

The freshness of the morning symbolized the newness of the couple's marriage as they began their life together. Interestingly, her sister Cynthia, unable to attend the ceremony because of her late stage pregnancy, called Sue to tell her that she had dreamed of a hot air balloon across the pond. Was it merely a coincidence that one drifted by moments after the ceremony?

Ghost Story
Lauren Allen

All rain is a ghost story
when dust rises to sky
that water is a whisper
is a rumor July started.

All rain is a ghost story
of rain, only horses who
gallop the serpentine
of the dead-end dirt road

plant their hoof prints
without thunder or lightning.
A past rain is the worst rain,
misunderstanding history

regardless of cracked earth.
What is maybe hot or is
definitely warm, births
impassible desert before August.

Everyone knows: to kill
a rattlesnake only when
they are crowded
outside of summer. Kill

all snakes under the full moon.
Burning like September
departs to the old barn
to multiply tangled weeds,

when no glistening rider
silently mouthing the true story,
under the rain in the sand,
rides again on the old trail.

Silently mouthing the true story,
the burning before we won't be
ghosts—freed by whispers,
the pop and hiss of October fire.

The Gardener
Kathryn Etters Lovatt

Sweat of a morning's weeding soaks through
his yellow shirt and makes him rise, a dry stalk
among bold shoots, staked vines, companion plants.
He rattles salt from his thinning bones as if
he could shake the burn of hard work and time.

A scarecrow stretch draws him sunward,
spins him till he settles down at boyhood.
Tranquility of smoked bees, sharp grasses, clouds
of apple blossoms: all gone now
to the seed of invisible fences, the three car garage.

He slips back to his task and into his habits,
memory and regret. How good the money sounded,
how hard the orchards fell.

White Flowers
Bobbi Adams

White flowers are not my favorites, but at the moment there seems to be nothing but white flowers in bloom in the garden. My first flush of roses is finished. How I will miss that wonderful cabbage rose, *Zephirine drouhin*, which is a rich pink, heavy with fragrance.

Let me begin a journey through the garden at the front of the yard on the street. First, you will meet a large native hydrangea, the oakleaf, *Hydrangea quercifolia*. The plant is large and flowers are white. I notice that I failed to completely remove spent flowers, now brown, from last year. Leave spent flowers on hydrangeas over winter. Old flowers protect new flowers from freeze during cold winters.

Also in that same bed, which holds all my air-layered camellia favorites from the James House, is a miniature cultivar of the larger native oakleaf. PeeWee stays low, but the flowers on both plants are identical. These plants look wonderful in winter as the exfoliating bark is more clearly seen when leaves fall off.

Under the large oakleaf plant lies one of my favorite native ground covers. *Michella repens*, partridge berry, is adorned in pairs of tiny white tubular flowers. The flowers join at the base to make a single red berry. Unfortunately, no partridge frequent my yard.

In front of the house, another native plant, *Itea virginica*, Virginia willow, is also in white flower. Sadly, this plant clones.

Despite willow in its common name, the plant under a kitchen window is not watered unless it rains. In fall turning leaves are pale yellow. In autumn, I prefer the plant for just this reason. Soon, however, this willow will be used as a trellis for *Passionata incarnate*. Maypop will be propped all over Virginia willow's limbs. The shrub seems unaffected by its use as a trellis and comes back strongly each spring with white flowers before maypop comes out of the ground.

In the pool, another white native, *Saururus cermes*, or lizard's tail, blooms. The common name describes the white flower which indeed looks like the upside down tails of lizards and geckos that run up and down the walls of the house and along the fence. Above the lizard's tail, a viburnum that likes wet feet is almost bloomed out. A cutting was moved to my garden from the flowing well along Highway 15 North. Viburnums along with dogwoods and maples have opposite twigs and are easily identified for that reason. As far as I know all viburnums, and I've three, have white flowers. Even *Viburnum plicatum maresii,* whose flowers look more like lace cap hydrangeas, has white flowers. I've lost this cultivar, unfortunately.

Mapleleaf viburnum, the leaves resemble those of maples, is also finished. All viburnums show marvelous color in the fall, when I like these plants the best. I especially like the *Mapleleaf viburnum* with yellow to orange leaves.

Climbing the bald cypress in the pool is a large vine. *Decumaria barbara,* a climbing hydrangea, has clusters of large, fragrant white flowers. Alas, these flowers are usually too high up for me to smell. Once in a while, the piece of the plant attached to

Halesia caroliniana, is low enough for my nose's enjoyment. Halesia also has white bell-shaped flowers that hang down. Carolina silverbell is the common name. I was fortunate enough to see a cultivar with many smaller flowers in bloom recently in Swan Lake Iris Gardens.

At the very back of the garden, on a large iron trellis, grows Asiatic jasmine. The flowers appear all summer long and are highly fragrant. Like climbing hydrangea, the jasmine must climb to bloom. I must say a white flowered garden at night under moonlight is very romantic. Try strolling though a garden of fragrant white flowers with the moon full overhead. Just do not forget Deep Woods OFF or mosquitoes will carry you off.

PHOTOGRAPH BY BOBBI ADAMS

Out of Ashes
Nick West

One Friday in February, 1979, my wife Ann and I did all the last minute things that everyone does before leaving for a vacation. We double-checked our lists, tried the windows, set the thermostat. We took one final look around before we locked the door behind us.

With our friends, Robert and June Jennings, we began to make our way toward overnights in Atlanta and Biloxi before arriving at our final destination, New Orleans. We had planned ten days of great food and sightseeing.

Despite the cold, we immersed our senses in the aromas and excitement of this coastal city. At The Gumbo House, we dined on seafood with Cajun seasoning before heading down Bourbon Street. Eventually, we found ourselves in Pat O'Brien's Bar. We enjoyed their famous Hurricanes until midnight.

We returned to our hotel, and once in bed, I quickly faded into the deep sleep of tall drinks and a full day of fun. When the phone rang five hours later, I might have still been in bit of a stupor as I rolled over and lifted the receiver, but I was anxious, too. In my mind, a phone call in the night meant bad news, and this was no exception. My wife's mother, back in Bishopville was on the other end of the line.

"Y'all's house is on fire right now!" she exclaimed. "We got a call from Nina Smith and she said it's about to burn to the ground."

I sat up straight in the bed, numb at such devastating news. "How did it happen?" was all I could manage to say.

"We don't know anything except the house and cars are on fire."

My wife rolled over. "Is Dad okay?" she asked.

I handed her the receiver. She soon hung the phone up and looked at me, tears streaming down her cheeks. "Oh, Nick," she said. "What are we going to do?"

While Ann went to wake our friends, I called Delta. The earliest flight out was at 7:30 a.m., two hours away. In less than thirty minutes, Robert was driving us to the airport. Once there, we moved through the terminal and boarded our flight to Columbia. As we awaited takeoff, thoughts of what we lost came pouring over both of us. We had not only lost our house, but possibly everything we'd accumulated for the past fifteen years. We didn't know where we would live or what, if anything, would be left to take with us to a new home.

Ann began to think of pictures, antiques, a sterling silver service set, cut glass pieces, jewelry, and, yes, her wedding dress that she had saved for our daughters. The distant sunlight through the glass window of the plane showed me she had already started the process of grieving, but within a few minutes, she turned and smiled at me. "At least we are all safe," she said.

My parents came to Columbia to pick us up. I first saw the sadness in their faces, but there were the kids, right behind them, running toward us. Ann and I dropped to the floor and hugged them and kissed them. None of us could control our emotions.

Our two daughters, 11 and 12, and our son, 10, had stayed with friends back home while we took our holiday. Ann had worried on the plane that they might have already seen the house. We both knew that the children felt as homeless and anxious as we did.

FOUR COLUMNS

Little conversation took place as Dad drove us back to Wisacky, the small community where we live. A mile away, as we topped a hill, we spotted a smoky haze coming from where the house once stood. As we got closer, we could see that the entire house was lost, not a single chimney survived, but the four huge white columns across the front of the house still stood like silent sentinels. They rose skyward some thirty feet into the air, just as they did in 1835, when Dr. Crane had them erected.

The house, in the typical antebellum style, was large: 5500 square feet. It had thirty-nine windows, four fireplaces, and sixteen-foot ceilings. The sills were hand-pegged and made of heart pine, and the flooring was all heart pine. Later we found out that the columns were constructed with bricks around the outside. Concrete was poured inside and in each column were four buggy axles and a dozen or so buggy springs scattered up and down the columns. Steel rebar wasn't invented until 1849.

Dad drove to the back, where our house used to be, and my parents stepped aside so we could survey the ruins on our own. Ann and the kids and I got out and walked through the ashes, our feet making crunching sounds with every step. The ashes smelled musty from all the water that soaked them.

I stopped where my closet had been and found the remains of my Browning and Remington shotguns. The stocks and foregrips were burned off; the metal was warped and twisted. Quail, dove, and duck hunts rushed into my mind from years ago. I had hunted with these guns since I was thirteen years old. One day I had hoped to pass them down to my son.

The children scattered to where each of their rooms were, looking for something that survived, but the fire left absolutely nothing. While Ann was looking in the dining room for any trace of her sterling silver service, or maybe a piece of cut glass, my oldest daughter walked up to her. "All of my Madam Alexander dolls are gone," she told her mother.

Angela chimed in, "All of my dolls are gone, too."

"Where is Jap?' my son suddenly asked.

Jap was our German Shepherd. Matt walked off calling the dog's name, but soon he returned with a question: "Do you think Jap burned up? He might have been under the house."

"He would have gotten out," I assured him. My employees were coming to feed and water our pet while we were gone, so I knew Jap had been looked after. "We'll find him."

Ann and I and the three children gathered in the area where the living room used to be and together we went out past the huge columns. We stopped and looked back at the carnage. I put my arms around the kids.

"We've all lost everything that we had," I said. "A part of our life is over, but we have each other, and we have the future."

The five of us walked out of the ashes that day, and we have never looked back. Well, a little now and then.

The next morning I returned and spent most of the day looking through the ashes for our dog's skeleton with a seed fork. He wasn't there. I searched the woods and never found his remains. He loved riding in the back of my pickup, and it occurred to me that, in a panic, maybe he jumped into the back of someone's truck. I thought it possible that he was safe somewhere in a good, new home. That's what we all hoped, and that is how we moved forward.

We built back exactly where the old house had been, and we have lived in that house now for thirty-five good years.

ANGELS IN UNLIKELY PLACES

Quaker Cemetery

   Be not forgetful to entertain strangers: for thereby some have entertained angels unawares.

Hebrews 13:2, King James Bible

Angels in Unlikely Places
Martha Dabbs Greenway

My brother was no angel and yet angels were everywhere at his funeral.

His name was Mac. He was almost eight years older than me. I wasn't sure he even knew my name until I was a teenager and he actually expressed concern about my dating one of his friends. In the last years of his life, we enjoyed a close friendship. One of his favorite philosophies was: "You can stay home for a week and remember nothing or take a trip and gain memories for a lifetime."

And, travel he did—a motorcycle while still in high school, an F86D jet fighter plane in the Air Force, a cool looking El Camino pick-up truck to run his golf course. A man on the move, one of his last joys was a huge black Harley Davidson motorcycle. "You pay a lot of money for a sound like this," he once told me as he revved up the engine ready for another adventure on the road.

But, back to the angels and his funeral.

The night before the service his family and I were doing what families do at such times—tell stories and enjoy the occasional outburst of healing laughter. When someone mentioned that Mac had given Harley jackets to his three grandsons for Christmas, they began to say with bravado, "Let's wear them to the funeral." I chimed in to say that I had a Harley jacket too, one my friend Peggy spotted at a thrift shop and bought for me. "Yeah, let's wear them!"

The next day I stood in my conservative gray Land's End dress when the oldest grandchild sidled up to me and asked, "Aunt Mar, are you really going to wear your jacket?" I knew it was a most important, fish or cut bait, defining moment and with only a slight hesitation I replied, "Yes, I am because Mac would have wanted me to follow my heart."

I'm sure there were murmured comments when those three young men and their 63-year-old, gray-haired great aunt entered the church but only one person approached me following the service, "Uh, are you wearing that jacket—hmmm—because of your brother?" I wanted to say something like, "Hell no. I wear this to all funerals," but refrained and simply said, "Yes, of course."

And, what does this have to do with angels? The Harley Davidson logo on our jackets looked like an angel's wing. Mac's middle child had ridden the Harley out and parked it beside the cemetery gate. Someone had placed a single red rose on the seat. More angel wings in the logos on the bike.

After the graveyard service, as we came out from under the funeral home tent, two people, separately, came up to me and gushed, "Did you see it? The clouds formed perfect angel wings. They came out of a clear blue sky and were visible through the entire service. Then they vanished!"

I wish I had seen those clouds but the final angel winged its way later that evening and it seemed to be just for me. We had opened my house for visitation and there were just two friends left chatting in the kitchen when I took a phone call and wandered into the living room while talking. What I saw there was most amazing. We had lit candles throughout the house. On the coffee table was a brass candle holder with a shield around its back side. The candle had melted in the shape of an angel's wing.

I suppose a pragmatist would explain it with "the candle leaned against the shield and the wax had nowhere to go but to build up on the sides of the candle."

To me it was one more message from an unlikely angel.

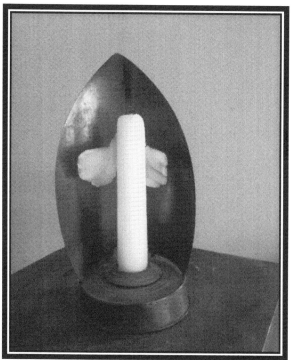

MAC'S CANDLE

quiltgift2001
Laura Bruno Lilly

Dedicated to those who are in need of a quiltgift and those who provide these works of (he)art.

from-Swimming with Swans: vignettes of our three year journey
between homes
July 2011 (the desert outside Las Cruces, NM)

One Christmas, I made and gave a quilt to a special person who was experiencing a period of extreme grief, hoping my creative handiwork would provide some solace. I found it easy to part with my artistic endeavor, trusting the new owner would enjoy it. I feel the same way when performing as a musician.

Recently, the quilt unexpectedly came back into my possession. This turn of events has offered me a unique opportunity to see my quilt in a different light. It has yielded unexpected insights into the person I was then, who I am now, and what I've learned in between times.

When it was returned, I first viewed it as an artistic piece. I was surprised to discern that I did not like it as my quilting style has changed significantly, more than I thought. It clearly showed a point in my life from which I have evolved, similar to what I and other musicians experience when we hear a recording made some time past. It surprised me to see this tangible evidence of where I had once been as a quilter.

Then, I began to remember the circumstances that prompted me to offer this person a comfort gift. Foremost, I recalled the deep need that drove me to give of myself in a nonverbal way, pouring out my heart-love during the process of making it. The quilt brought back the memory of offering prayers, crying tears with each stitch, and knowing it was not only cathartic for me in its making, but a symbolic gesture in the giving of it.

Also, I remember trying to tame my "crazy-scrap-quilt" style, shaping it into something more "palatable" to this person's tastes and trying to tone down my own bolder color palette for their more subdued powder baby blues preferences. In so doing, I think it diminished the quilt's artistic value, but not its worth as a gift of love and compassion.

What I think I've learned in the interim is an ability to incorporate others' preferences more easily into a piece, presentation, or gift of which I can be proud. I do so when, as a musician, I gear programs, concerts, or performances towards a particular audience. It's a smart thing to do. The trick is to give 'em what they want with a twist....an appropriate twist, but a twist just the same. Examples of what I've done is to include one of my own arrangements of a Celtic piece for solo classical guitar into an otherwise traditional setting or by playing a wildly exciting 20th century classical guitar piece in a program filled with standard fare, fluff.

The following seems to sum up the above while giving it greater credence given its famous and honored author. It also reminds me of the conversations we often have with each other as colleagues.

"The Two Poems"

by Kahlil Gibran,
The Wanderer: His Parables and His Sayings

Many centuries ago, on a road to Athens, two poets met, and they were glad to see one another.

And one poet asked the other saying, "What have you composed of late, and how goes it with your lyre?"

And the other poet answered and said with pride, "I have but now finished the greatest of my poems, perchance the greatest poem yet written in Greek. It is an invocation to Zeus the Supreme."

Then he took from beneath his cloak a parchment, saying, "Here, behold, I have it with me, and I would fain read it to you. Come, let us sit in the shade of that white cypress."

And the poet read his poem. And it was a long poem.

And the other poet said in kindliness, "This is a great poem. It will live through the ages, and in it you shall be glorified."

And the first poet said calmly, "And what have you been writing these late days?"

And the other answered, "I have written but little. Only eight lines in remembrance of a child playing in the garden." And he recited the lines.

The first poet said, "Not so bad; not so bad."

And they parted.

And now after two thousand years the eight lines of the one poet are read in every tongue, and are loved and cherished.

And though the other poem has indeed come down through the ages in libraries and in the cells of scholars, and though it is remembered, it is neither loved nor read.

ANTIQUE QUILT

The Look
MARTHA DABBS GREENWAY

There's nothing worse
than receiving The Look
when you least need it.

I'm trying to get through each day
then you remind me.
There's such a difference in *How're you doin'?*
and *How are you?* said with hand touching heart.

They usually add something like
You sure do look good.
One day I won't ask myself
What were they expecting?

Yes, I should be grateful that they care
Yes, I understand they mean well
Yes, I've done it myself.

THE COOLING COUCH
Bobbi Adams

What is a "cooling couch"? Isabelle McCutchen, my across-the-street neighbor, and I had a conversation about just such a piece of furniture this morning. The first time I heard the expression Jewell Tindall (another Bishopville friend) informed me that one of the ugliest pieces of furniture I have ever seen, an Empire-style couch at the James House, home of the Lee County Historical Society, is a "cooling couch." This couch is heavy, massive with a very narrow bench seat – its red velvet cover faded to pink. There are moth holes in the velvet.

Originally given to the S.C. Cotton Museum, the sofa made its way to the James House. It was carried upstairs and put out of sight. This ugly piece of furniture seems very masculine to me. Indeed, it came from the estate of "Cotton Ed" Smith, the longest serving senator from South Carolina before Strom Thurmond broke his record. The couch is much too narrow, for example, for me to rest on. My hips are too broad. I would roll right off onto the floor.

Jewell Tindall first found this musty sofa in an antique store. Its original purpose, I am told, was to lay out the dead in the parlor, a seldom used room in northern and southern antebellum houses. Doors to the parlor are normally kept closed. The room is opened up after a family death and the body is laid out. "Cotton Ed" was placed on this couch when he died and his family held his wake in his Lynchburg home, Tanglewood. Drinks were served all around as people visited with each other around the body.

Now fast forward in time to the year 2008. Too heavy to move, the couch is left in place when the plasterers come to restore the walls of the James House. The couch is covered with heavy plastic to protect it. It is after all a gift to the Historical Society. The new plaster mildews in the unheated house. Green, yellow, and black mold grow on the newly-finished walls. The contractor is called back to correct the mold issues.

His solution: sand out the damage, cut out the worst places, replaster the damage and everything will be fine.

Everything is not fine. Dust seeps everywhere, including underneath the plastic furniture covers and into the office, exempt from the plaster contract. It also seeps into the ugly couch.

Negotiations begin between lawyers. We go back and forth. The Historical Society finally signs off on a rebate of $3000 from a contract of $27,000. The money is to be paid back in $1000 increments by June 2010. The plasterer agrees only to recover the furniture that was damaged. It is still necessary to raise $64,000 for another plaster job. We divorce our lawyers but still must find money to completely redo the walls in the two-story James House.

Our ugly couch goes off to an upholsterer. Stripes of blue, gold, and red replace faded velvet. Our couch is brought back from the dead. It is to be placed downstairs in a place of honor in the library with drapes to match. The room will be painted yellow. Yellow brightens the dark rooms of the James House, whose windows are shaded by porch and trees. Gone is the spectre of death in faded velvet. Now we have a handsome piece of Empire furniture.

Life is like that couch. "La petite mort." I did not see death coming this time. It pricked me three times before here in Bishopville. My body knew "la petite mort" was coming again. The third eye (my intuition) saw it. I need to increase blood flow. Red is the color of menstruation, of maturation, of life. I must get my wild horse out again. Yet I resist.

Starting over (beginning again), I hate doing things twice, much less three times. Yet after death comes the resurrection. Slowly I am pulling out of the abyss, looking for color in blackness. Black is not found in tubes of paint. It is made by mixing red, blue and yellow. I don't have black on my artist's palette. Like the recovered couch, colors are there in blue, red and yellow, the primaries. White only fades color, turning it grey. Although we are moving into fall and winter, I am back in springtime when sap rises again and new life flows.

Energy comes from the mind not the body. I will remember that daily. As the external body fades to dusty pink—red, the color of blood and of life, still rises in my veins. The sky is still blue, flowers yellow.

Wash
Kathryn Etters Lovatt

Under this sun, the ghost of my grandmother appears;
my mother follows, a shimmer in her wake.
The two stand ankle-deep in nettles and wicker baskets.
Their teeth are clothespins.

They move down the line in unison
pitching tails of bleached sheets skyward.
A snatch of their wrists seeds the day with billow;
the world turns to dreams and white percale.

Unborn beneath a skein of bees and mimosa,
I wait for the clear blue of August to pass,
wait for the wind-bearing lungs of autumn,
for the harvest of amber honey and myself.

My mothers will fetch me once they're done.
They will finish here and come and lift
the thought of me into the folds of their aprons.
They will take me home.

Even now, their pocket charms sing in my ear:
river rock, pulley-bone,
blade and spoon.
Nothing has begun yet, and nothing is over.

Garden of Memories
Bobbi Adams

It should come as no surprise that I am not a southern lady. I am told that often enough. My accent gives me away even after 38 years in the south. As for the lady part, ladies do not sweat, they perspire. I am here to tell you that I sweat. Get behind a push mower in June, July and August in the shade, when the heat index is supposed to reach 110, and you will sweat too.

I like to do my own yard work—mowing, pulling weeds, edging, dead-heading flowers. The dome of green in my garden covers me like the domes of basilicas in Venice, where I did the first two years of my master's degree in studio art from New York University. I started each morning in Venice, worshipping in front of Titian's masterpiece over the high altar in the Frari. On alternate days I sat in front of the Bellini Madonna in the Lady Chapel of the same church.

Here at home, in an impoverished Southern county with a declining population (no jobs), my garden is church. In this church I sweat away bad thoughts, sweat away worries, come in and take a shower and feel absolutely happy. It doesn't take much to please me anymore at my age. Bring me a flower or plant I've never seen before and you will be remembered in my garden forever.

I know my late husband's cousin will not remember that she brought a plant to him found along a power line in Columbia along which she was riding. I knew what it was instantly because in the North, this plant, Jerusalem cherry, is a house plant, often given as a gift at Christmas. The orange fruit is not edible and the plant will not survive outside above the Mason-Dixon Line. Now, however, it is growing in my garden, in shade, in sun, along the driveway, in the gravel, in pot plants. You could say it is become a pest. The leaves have quite a pungent scent I actually like. Whenever I find it somewhere I do not desire, I pull it up. Along the edge of the driveway by the side of the kitchen, the soil is pretty inhospitable. Not even perennial *Vinca major* likes it there, but Jerusalem cherry thrives and survives the winter. Warmed by the sun on the kitchen wall it keeps growing, blooming, and fruiting.

Life lessons are learned from the garden. Pushing the lawnmower sweats out soul darkness and puts it back into the soil. My temper definitely improves. I can't stay angry or upset with anyone after pushing a lawnmower. This is especially true since I have given away all my own lawnmowers, which seemed never to stay operable. Oh yes, I learned to change sparkplugs, change oil, change wheels. Yet every spring would find me struggling to get the "consarned" things to start. Finally friends took pity on me. One carted two inoperable mowers away. He can use the parts. The second friend loans me his mower when I need it and thus he is responsible for maintenance. I supply the gas and leave him with gas in the tank. All I have to do is give one tug and away we go to sweat out impurities. After I shower and clean-up, I sit down by my pool and count fish, completely happy. The yard always looks better when it is trimmed up. I feel better as well.

New things are discovered every day by gardening. Buds appear on plants. Ephemeral wildflowers such as blood root suddenly appear as I go looking with a cup of coffee in hand. Surprises appear in pots along the split rail fence. White hyacinths are showing buds. Usually I do not like white flowers. They look too perfect, which I am not, but these hyacinths look and smell wonderful.

For many years blue and pink hyacinths appeared in the garden, given to my mother around Easter when she was living with me at the end of her life. After a while I realized that hyacinths quite like me and take no maintenance on my part, like the lawnmower borrowed from a friend.

I visit friends in my garden. The hyacinths remind me of mother. Plants given to me by other gardeners remind me of their friendships. My garden is also a garden of memories.

My husband and I planted *Decumaria barbara* and *Halesia caroliniana* next to each other in the garden. *Barbara and Hal planted together Christmas Day in 1976.* Decumaria does not bloom unless it climbs, which it is now doing up the bald cypress in the pool, by the side of which I rest after mowing.

I drink coffee and count fish.

Death and Dinner
Brenda Bevan Remmes

There are people you love most of the time and those whom you adore all of the time. But then there is a rare circle of characters who are so charming, so original, so unforgettable that you not only enjoy them in

advance but continue to laugh with absolute affection, even after they're gone. That was my Uncle Gene and Aunt Nell.

He was a military man, who raised four boys in regimented fashion; she, the daughter of a Methodist minister, was partial to varying shades of red hair and long tight skirts. When the boys had all left home she had an epiphany her life should be more pink. What followed was a complete renovation of their house and wardrobe. Everything became pink. I say this not as whimsical touches of table cloths and dishes. I literally mean rugs, curtains, furniture, all bathroom accessories and clothes, from underwear outward. I can't attest to the fact that Uncle Gene's underwear was pink, but knowing Aunt Nell if I had to bet I'd give her the upper hand. Like an old war house, he took orders well and he, like everyone else, adored her.

A second epiphany she'd had when the boys left home was that it was no longer necessary to cook. They ate out every meal, dressed in coordinated pink outfits. Breakfast every morning was at Bojangles, then the afternoon and evening meals varied depending on the day of the week. My husband and I always joined them on Friday nights at The Compass, a local fish place. To watch them enter a room was worth the price of the meal.

They had become regulars at their favorite restaurants and many people knew them. But even those who didn't would stop and look up when the doors opened and they entered: bright red hair, large pink sunglasses and a tremendous rose cloth flower always pinned to her bodice. Her arm was slipped into the hook of his elbow. He wore a pink shirt with matching socks and a red or purple tie. His pants were sometimes white, in the winter more often black. Heads turned and the room would become quiet as they made their way arm in arm across the floor. She had a bad hip and limped. He was bent with age and shuffled. But they shared smiles with everyone and waved and even those who didn't know them would wave in return as if they were the Duke and Duchess of Earl.

Sadly, Nell died in 2005. Uncle Gene's health began to decline immediately. Family and friends tried to keep him on his regular outings for lunch and dinner. When he stopped wearing his pink shirts we should have known immediately. We had talked him into joining us at the Compass one Friday night and his son agreed to drive him over. When he came in, his head was bent, his skin pallid. "How you doin', Uncle Gene," I asked as we helped him into a chair.

"Dubious," he said.

My mother sat down across from him and took his hands in hers. "You don't look like you feel too well," she said. He didn't respond, but shortly he appeared to doze off and you could hear the slight murmur of a soft snore.

"His hands are cold," mother said.

"All the time, any more," his son, Rees, said. "They stay cold."

"Shall we order for him?"

"Go ahead. He'll wake back up when the food gets here."As if nothing were different we chatted away, ourselves and three other cousins: reviewed the week's happenings, caught up on the doings of a few relatives. When the food arrived, Rees was unable to rouse his father.

"Perhaps we should get them to pack up everything and we'll take it back to his house. He might want to lie down," I said. The waitress removed the plates to accommodate us.

"Daddy," Rees said. "Daddy, we're going to take you home. I'm going to pull the car around and we'll eat at home instead."

Gene did not answer, his head still bowed. Rees gave his father a good shake and pulled his head back. Once I saw the deep blue tinges of his lips and his eyes rolled back into the sockets, I knew at once he was dead.

"Uncle Gene's dead, I do believe," I finally said out loud.

"Oh no, not here in this place. Not now," my mother said horrified.

No one said a word. Rees let his father's head rest back on the table and we all sat motionless for a moment while the waitress returned our food all bagged up in Styrofoam and ready to go. "Anything else," she asked in a cherry voice.

"Nothing at the moment," I said.

Finally Rees broke the silence. "How are we going to get him out of here?"

Another cousin piped up. "You get him under one arm and I'll get him under the other. I think we could do it."

"A wheel chair would be easier. See anyone with a wheel chair we could borrow?" mother said.

We took a gander around the crowded restaurant. All tables were filled. A line 25 people deep stood in the doorway of the entrance. It was going to be tough to fool this crowd, but such a shame to ruin everyone's dinner by having someone die in the middle of it.

"We could call the rescue squad."

"They make such a scene," Mother said. "They'll hurl him to the floor, rip open his shirt, stuff a tube down his throat. Nasty stuff. It'll all look nasty."

"Would definitely mess up everyone's dinner," I added.

"Let's go for trying to carry him out," my cousins agreed.

Almost as the decision was made, sirens wailed in the background. Four men with stretchers came hurdling past the patrons at the door to the complete surprise of the hostess. As we knew they would, they dropped Uncle Gene to the floor, tore open his shirt and immediately began CPR. Everything in the restaurant stopped.

"Who called them?" I said in disgust as I looked up at the front door and saw my husband shrug his shoulders and raise his cell phone. I should have known. He's from Iowa; so practical, so logical about his approach to life and death. I made my way through the crowd. "Why did you do that?"

"Maybe he wasn't dead," he said. "It seemed like the thing to do."

Murmurs of "he's dead," began rippling through the restaurant as the rescue guys loaded the body on the stretcher and moved to the ambulance. I gave my husband my best "I-told-you-so" glare and headed to get mother.

"I think we could have handled that better," Mother said. "It didn't have to be such an event."

My cousins were paying the bill and packing up the boxes of food as we made our way to the door. "We'll follow the ambulance to the hospital," I suggested.

She nodded her head in agreement as tears began to appear. "We could have classed it up a bit for him, don't you think? I'm just so sorry this didn't happen at the Country Club instead."

It Was in Motion: XIII Ways to Remember My Hair

Martha Dabbs Greenway

I
My hair looked like a silver river, snaking down the black folds of the cape. Snip, snip, snip,

II
Wisps of dandelion seed-pods, poof, blown to the sky.

III
Stillness, inert, dead protein until the whisk, whisk of the broom swept it again into motion.

IV
If I thought that was short, short began when Louie, armed now with electric clippers, began the systematic uncovering of my scalp: zzzzzz, zzzzzz.

V
Ann called me Woodstock before; now, I guess she'll call me G.I. Jane.

VI
Bare-headed in the restaurant, the grocery store, the bank, the hardware store.

VII
Donna waved and thanked me for a thank you note.
Pam smiled and gave a thumbs up.
Jeff offered two baseball hats.

VIII
When I first saw that gray hair on the shelf at the wig shop, I thought, *witch's hair*. Then Mary-Brent picked it up and said, "This is you." Damned if it wasn't.

IX

Later, my friend from college, the one who always gives good advice, told me, "Get a wig with a few more dark hairs. Bet it'd take off some years. Here," she said, and handed me directions to her favorite shop.

X

Until age thirty-three, my almost black hair fought off the gray. I dismissed even highlights so I never thought this would happen.

XI

"Going blonde" wasn't even in the picture until the lady at Elegante Wig Shop plopped that longish blonde wig on me. My eyes widened. Friends now look at me and then look again.

XII

I thought I was "in disguise" but most called my name, commented on how good I looked (I wonder what they were expecting?), a few, bless their hearts, seemed shocked it wasn't my real hair.

XIII

The next chapter? I don't know yet.

Perpetual Care
Kathryn Etters Lovatt

Stranger, who sleeps by my mother,
I bring rosemary and a stone
scrubbed in the holy waters of my father's brook.
I pull crab and sour grass off your shoulders,
smooth the earth, newly turned and tamped,
filling the space beside you.
I speak your Christian name.

If the memory of your mortal hand
extends beyond this plotted underworld,
if you hold power beyond this spell,
reach beyond sense and reason
until one unencumbered finger
takes root and rises, a flowering vine
beneath your neighbor's feet.

CONTRIBUTORS

Bobbi Adams is professional artist, master gardener emeritus, and master naturalist. She writes a weekly column for her local newspaper called the Peripatetic Gardener. From these columns came her first book, *Gatherings from the Garden,* published in 2013. The second volume came out in October of 2014.

Lauren Allen is a professional horse trainer and is earning her Master of Fine Arts degree in Creative Nonfiction at The University of South Carolina. She is a Pushcart Prize nominated poet and Winner of the South Carolina Writers' Workshop Carrie McCray Awards in Poetry and Nonfiction.

Paddy Bell's first writing endeavor, *DOGS: The Musical,* was produced in several venues, culminating in a run at the renowned Piccolo Spoleto Arts Festival and the production of a musical CD. This success launched a writing interest that spans the genres of screenplay, short story, and children's literature. She is currently working on a series of children's picture books and her father's World War II story. She has been published in *The Petigru Review,* South Carolina Literary Anthology.

Mindy Blakely The International Library of Poetry published two of her poems, "Alone Again" and "First Kiss" in their anthologies titled *Outstanding Poets of 1998* and *Traces of Yesterday,* both released in 1998. An avid reader of mysteries and romance stories, Blakely also holds a Bachelor of Science degree in Business Administration from Winthrop College in Rock Hill, SC.

Jayne Bowers, a semi-retired educator with the SC Education System, has published articles in *Guideposts*, *The Petigru Review,* and two LDS magazines, the *Ensign* and the *Liahona.* She is the author of *Human Relations in Industry* (Jayne Crolley), *Musings of a Missionary Mom, Eve's Sisters,* and *Crossing the Bridge: Succeeding in a Community College and Beyond. Jayne's favorite blog is www.jaynebowers.wordpress.*

Ari Dickinson began writing as a child when she needed appropriate plays and musicals to direct for her siblings and their friends. She wrote the book and lyrics for a musical which was produced in Tennessee, and the libretto for a one-act opera which was a finalist in the New York City Opera Competition. Her articles have been published in *Dance Teacher Now* and *Dance Spirit* Magazine, and her poetry has been published in *Virtue.*

Vanessa Friedrich is a professional equestrian and native German who has lived in the United States since 2002. After recovering from a severe horse riding accident, she wrote her first book, *Determination or Just Plain Stubbornness.* An excerpt from this book was published in a recent volume of *Chicken Soup.* Vanessa is a therapeutic riding instructor and equine specialist.

Martha Dabbs Greenway is a seventh generation South Carolinian, and resides at Dabbs Crossroads in a rambling country farm house built by her granddaddy. Co-founder of the Southern Sampler Artists Colony and retired Director of the Sumter County Cultural Commission, Martha lives contentedly with her cats, Sonoma, rescued on the Northern California coast, and an orange tabby named Salem, who showed up on her porch, while she was reading about an orange cat dropped off at a library in Iowa.

Laura Bruno Lilly was born into a family of musicians and artists. Nurtured and surrounded by several generations and genres of music and the arts, writing has been a faithful companion. Her articles and reviews have appeared in publications such as *The Rosette, The Mandolin Journal,* and the *GFA Soundboard.* Laura is currently working on two novels and a book of creative non-fiction. Originally from Colorado, she is new to the Camden SCWW chapter. www.laurabrunolilly.com

Kathryn Etters Lovatt, a Camden resident, earned her MA in creative writing from Hollins University. A former winner of the Doris Betts Prize, she also won Press 53's short fiction competition in 2012 and again in 2013. Both her fiction and poetry have been nominated for Pushcart prizes. A Virginia Center for the Creative Arts fellow, she received South Carolina Art Commission's Individual Artist Fellowship for prose in 2013.

Brenda Bevan Remmes lives near the Black River Swamp in South Carolina in an old family home filled with the history of generations past. Her debut novel, *The Quaker Café,* was published in March of 2014 by Inkwell Publishing, New York, and purchased in August 2014 for worldwide distribution by Lake Union Publishing, Seattle. She is working on a sequel. www.brendaremmes.com

Nick West, a resident of Wisacky, South Carolina has published magazine articles to accompany his wildlife photography. He has been published in magazines such as *The Charleston Magazine, Water Dogs, Bloodlines*, and *Hunting and Fishing*.

Douglas Wyant has received a Scott Lax Wildacres Scholarship and a Carrie McCray Memorial Literary Award from South Carolina Writers' Workshop. His stories have been published in *HomeLife*, *The Petigru Review*, and *moonShine review*. A native of Camden, he lives in Kershaw County with his wife Gail.